Typographically Speaking

Alan Peckolick

teaching TYPE to TALK

With thoughts by Ivan Chermayeff, George Lois & Jan V. White

If you can read it, I can't do it

AP

Teaching TYPE To TALK

Editorial director: Suzanne Slesin

Design: Alan Peckolick & Dominick Santise, Jr.

Assistant editor: Deanna Kawitzky

POINTED LEAF PRESS, LLC.
WWW.POINTEDLEAFPRESS.COM

For Jessica, my navigator through all the storms, real and imagined

CONTENTS

A Note from Ivan Chermayeff 6

A Few Words from George Lois 9

Preface by Jan V. White 10

Introduction by Ina Saltz 14

1. Typographically Speaking 32

2. Radical Me 68

3. Hollywood Calling 88

4. Dealing with The Suits 112

5. In Your Face 146

Index 166

Acknowledgments 168

A Note from Ivan Chermayeff

I love type. To be more accurate, I love letters and numbers. There is no end to the expressiveness and all the connections that type can bring to ideas to make them resonate and echo and otherwise bring to life messages worth learning and repeating, with the hope that others will attach themselves to the particular words with the same enthusiasm.

The excitement of visual connections is what letter forms brought together in new, creative ways, enhances, enriches, and embellishes communications, to make them more meaningful, noticeable, and memorable.

"Expressive" is the term and feeling for the style that Alan Peckolick has brought to graphic design as it is practiced today. Alan is roughly of the same vintage as Tom Geismar and myself. We all started our professional lives in the late 1950s and established ourselves in the next two decades after that. We have all been working away ever since with our mutual love of type.

And, along with incredible changes in technology that have brought speed and flexibility and an array of choices to apply to the process of solving other people's communications problems, has also come a shift from thinking about the craft of commercial art to actually being in the business of developing visual ideas, which we now call "graphic design," without the necessity of explaining in too much detail what that means.

So much of graphic design (at least exceptional graphic design) is formed around ideas—looking at the meaning of words and finding ways to express them with excitement and originality.

In doing this, it is not abandoning the craft of old sign makers and lettering artists, but seriously appreciating what they did. People who invented things or grew things or made things that other people needed or wanted required someone else with the skills to get their ideas across. Hence graphic designers came into the picture.

I remember starting out after graduating from Yale and admiring Lou Dorfsman of CBS, and his friend Herb Lubalin, with whom I became very friendly when Lou was working for Sudler & Hennessey. (The two were *the* shining lights, doing the best of what was going on in graphic design.) I had started out, myself, at Columbia Records as one of several assistants to S. Neil Fujita in those years, and in the office of Alvin Lustig, while Alan learned at the side of Herb Lubalin.

Alan Peckolick has since then demonstrated on many occasions his ability to arrive at the core of a typographic symbol or logotype problem. His work on annual reports and logo design is particularly admirable.

—Ivan Chermayeff

In 1964, a pioneering legend in the modern graphic arts movement, Herb Lubalin interviewed Alan Peckolick, who had recently graduated from Pratt Institute, recognized his talent, and gave him a starting job. Young Alan, thrilled, worked as an assistant to the great master, and somehow, precociously, opened his own office. Alan was soon asked by Lubalin to rejoin him, eventually under the name Lubalin, Peckolick Associates—a Horatio Alger story if there ever was one. With his spectacular creative background, Peckolick has spent his life as a graphic communicator, driven by his love of the letterform, dazzling people's eyes and making type talk, magnificently.

—George Lois

Preface by Jan V. White

Art? Of course the sort of gorgeous graphic design that a virtuoso like Alan Peckolick has produced is art. How can you not see that when you flip through these coffee-table–sized pages? Dig deeper, though. Don't let all that visual beauty (yes, beauty) bamboozle you into thinking that splendor is all there is, and you are done.

Think about it: Where do these images and typography come from? How do they manage to create such impact and excitement? What are they for (beside being gorgeous)? They are each a brilliant solution to a specific problem that only seems to appear visual. They are far more than that, and the process of creating their form starts elsewhere—in their content. The problem originates from the client (few of them enlightened), who has a need that is intellectual, theoretical, and financial, and is always in a rush. In terms of "design," he is probably misguided. Furthermore, whatever plan is available is usually confused, amorphous, vague, and disorganized. Admit it: A mess. What to do? Call in an inexperienced hotshot who will camouflage it all, so it is neat, pretty, and startling. That is usually described by that word Creative.

Along comes that high-priced designer ("Hey, let's call Peckolick—he has a huge reputation, we ought to be safe hiring him") and he shows samples to knock your eyes out.

Then Peckolick sits there in the conference room, where he listens and slowly figures out what these confused and confusing clients are really talking about. He must divine what they really need. What are they selling and whom are they wanting to sell it to? What is their purpose? Realize that what it might possibly look like hasn't even been mentioned, because this sleuthing is not a bit artistic: It is seriously analytical. Perhaps you can simplify the process and just call it Thinking.

Why do these Peckolick solutions work? Not only do

they look great, but they also answer the specific intellectual needs that underlie those solutions, no matter the kind of project he may have on the board. (Not too many remember that image: We used to have great big wooden drawing boards, where we pushed pencils until markers came in...then we traced lettering by hand until Letraset was invented...and rubber cement that had that delicious "high" odor... Nostalgia. Oh, well!) No matter whether projects are about "Dealing with The Suits" or "Hollywood Calling," all have to be properly figured out. From that process slowly evolves the ideal design.

Hoping that a brilliant idea will come from Kissing the Muse seldom works. Remember Edison's truism about genius being 1% inspiration and 99% perspiration? He was right. It takes hard work to assemble all that mass of ideas, words, and visible stuff into the amalgam of "great graphic design." Just think of the choices of images, medium, symbols, typefaces, sizes, colors, white space, direction, and who-knows-what-else (aside from clients' predilections). It all has to come together in order to make sense. It grows organically out of the message and its functional purpose. Remarkably, that "sense-making" can also be simplified into a single defining term: Editing.

Great design is just as much the verbal solution to a specific problem as a visual solution to that same problem. Such verbal/visual communication (i.e., editing-together-with-designing) demands a blend of skills and attitude. It is so much more intuitive than just clever, startling visuals you say "Wow!" to. Intrinsic meaning makes the difference. Distinguished graphic design offers more than the "Wow!" factor because its meaning lasts while its appearance gives joy. That is why a whole book's-worth of Peckolick is such a great investment. You can sit and look, and think, and compare, and think, and turn the page, and think, and notice, and think, and study, and think, and learn, and think…

—Jan V. White

ALAN PECKOLICK

Introduction by Ina Saltz

From the mid-sixties through the early eighties, the hottest graphic design shop around was the one (under various names) headed by the prodigiously talented Herb Lubalin, aided by his equally talented protégé and later partner, Alan Peckolick. A revolution was happening in graphic design, just as a revolutionary spirit was taking hold in all areas of American culture. Known as "expressive typography" or "graphic expressionism," it was a movement characterized by a more informal organization of space, and conceptual typography that "solved" the problem visually.

■ The novelty of allowing the personality of the designer to come forward in presenting ideas, the need to design each piece uniquely, was radical in its time and, like many such ideas, gradually entered the mainstream.

■ Fortuitously, this movement coincided with the transformation of printing technology. Type had previously been set in metal, so it had been physically impossible

Alan in the late 1960s.

to make type touch or overlap. Every piece of metal had to sit next to another piece of metal: Space could be added between letters, but not "subtracted." With the advent of phototype, there were no physical barriers, and type could be set as closely as the designer wished by exposing a negative of the letters on a piece of film which was then developed, or drawn by hand.

■ Herb Lubalin and Alan Peckolick were the most visible of the proponents of expressive typography, and it became their visual trademark, affecting all of the work produced by their design office. Indeed, Lubalin has been called "the father of conceptual typography" by the eminent design critic Steven Heller. In 1971, Lubalin co-founded ITC, the International Typeface Corporation. The impact of his ideas was magnified when Lubalin started the magazine *U&lc*, a sales tool for ITC that also served as a visual outlet for his expressive ideas. It is hard to overestimate the influence of *U&lc* on the graphic design

"I got it all and I got it young"

world of the seventies. Suddenly, letters were twirling and doing somersaults, serving simultaneously as word, image, and idea.

■ The "marriage" of Lubalin and Peckolick was serendipitous, as well. Both loved letterform, loved wordplay, were obsessed with typographic possibility, and were irreverent. But if it were not for a chance meeting, this partnership that changed both men's lives and perhaps this chapter in the history of graphic design itself might never have happened.

■ Alan Peckolick's story began in 1940 in the Bronx, where he was born to letter carrier Charles Peckolick and his wife, Belle Binenbaum. Alan liked to draw as a child, and Belle urged him to go into "the city" to visit libraries and museums. When Alan was old enough to travel to Manhattan on his own, she sent him to visit the "Metropolitan Museum of Modern Art," confusing the names of two major museums. Alan went, reluctantly, and was soon in tears after going up and down on the bus, unable to find the museum.

■ "I liked to draw soldiers and cowboys, and things in the movies, at first," Alan says. "Then I fell in love with cars and drew them constantly, especially custom cars and hot rods."

■ Alan went to Elmont Memorial High School on Long Island. "I was the best artist in the school," he says. "I did all the posters for the dances and other events... most of the other boys wanted to be auto mechanics. I knew I wanted to go to art school, plus I knew I wouldn't get into any normal school because I graduated from high school by the skin of my teeth. I became an artist because if you can't spell and can't write and can't count and don't know grammar, a visual arts career is the only thing left," he says with a rueful smile.

At an industry conference in Hamburg, speaking to 300 German designers, Alan realized he was the only one in the room who spoke English.

"I now realize my career matured before I did"

■ "When it was time for college I put all of my drawings in a brown paper bag, as I'd never heard of a portfolio. This is what I took around for my 'applications.' Pratt Institute accepted me on a probational basis in illustration in their evening division. After three months, it became clear that it wasn't working out, and I was told that I should leave. I felt as if I had died. I went from being the most talented kid in my high school to a school where most of the kids were from the High School of Music and Art. I met a friend of mine in the coffee shop and he said, 'Why not switch to graphic design?' I said, 'What's graphic design?' He said, 'Don't worry about what it is, just remember that you don't have to know how to draw.' I plunged into the graphic design curriculum. My first instructor was Al Kator. He was a senior designer at CBS, a real wild man who spoke in words I had never heard before, terms like *balance, shape, form*. My first three years there were hell. My assignments were torn up in front of the class. I will never forget that in the first class he said, 'Some of you will wake up one morning and understand design, and some of you will never understand design.'"

■ "During the years I was going to school at night and working at agencies during the day, I discovered the film-title sequence work of Saul Bass, and fell madly in love with graphic design. In my senior year, my work changed 180 degrees. I did the best work in the class—half the work in the senior show was mine. However, I kept getting fired from my agency jobs because I cared how the page looked instead of caring about selling soap."

■ "I was going to California with some friends, and I asked a cousin of mine who was on the fringes of the movie business to find Saul Bass in California, and set up an appointment for me to meet with him. But when I arrived, the receptionist apologetically told me that Bass had had to go to New York City and would I mind showing my work to his right-

Judging D&AD in London sometime in the 1970s.

Alan discusses the future of typography at the International Typeface Corporation.

hand man, Art Goodman. Goodman spent an incredible two hours showing me around the studio and said how much he loved my work. He said that next time Bass came to New York, he'd call me for an interview. (I thought to myself: Bullshit.)"

■ "I went back to New York to work at McCann Erickson as a studio assistant, then spent six months in the Army Reserve, and forgot completely about Saul Bass. One year to the day from my interview with Art Goodman, I was in my office at McCann Erickson, and I got a call from my mother (I was still living at home) telling me that Bass was at the Plaza Hotel for the rest of the day and he wanted to meet me. I was overwhelmed. I ran up to meet with him that afternoon and we hit it off completely from a chemistry standpoint. He offered me a job in California, including living expenses and travel, all paid for—he was that enthusiastic about my work. When he returned to California, I got a call from him saying his financial people said it didn't make sense to spend all that money getting me out there when there was so much talent in California, but that he hoped we'd stay in touch. This was the beginning of a lifelong friendship."

■ "At this time in my life, I had two design heroes—Saul Bass and Herb Lubalin. Based on Saul's reaction to my work, he gave me the impetus to try to meet Herb Lubalin. Herb was impossible to reach because he was leaving Sudler & Hennessey and was about to open his own office. I was working for a small agency and calling Herb's office every day. Unbeknownst to me, a woman with whom I was working had previously worked with him; when she saw my work, she said I should meet Herb. I said I hadn't been able to reach him. She picked up the phone, dialed a number and said, 'Hello, Herb,' and the next thing I knew, I had an interview."

■ "The next day, with great trepidation, I went to Herb's new office, which was still under construction.

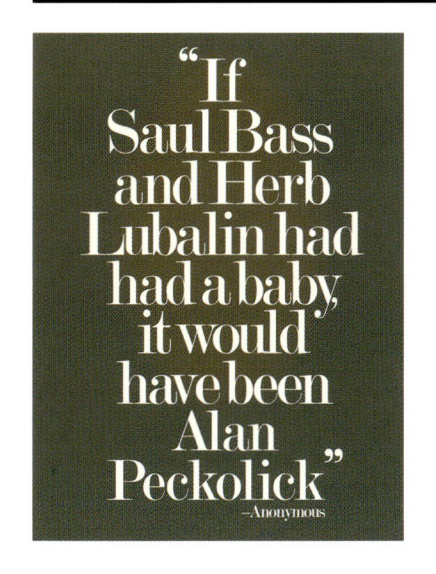

"If Saul Bass and Herb Lubalin had had a baby, it would have been Alan Peckolick"
—Anonymous

In 2010, the New York Type Directors Club surprised Alan with a poster honoring his legacy. Alan stole the poster.

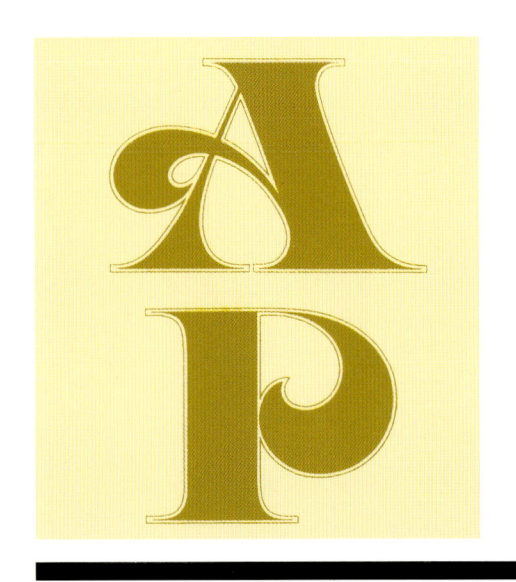

Alan Peckolick Graphic Design, 1969–1974.

Herb interviewed me by looking at my portfolio with his right hand while he was doing a layout with his left. After ten minutes, he closed the portfolio and asked if I'd like to be his assistant. And then my design education really began."

■ Peckolick started as Lubalin's assistant in 1963; he was 24 years old. "I was a very insecure person; I had no background in culture. I had been thrust into this situation with Lubalin, who knew about art, books, music. I was on a tremendous learning curve. The people at the office were light years ahead of me and I always felt I was playing catch-up. But when I went to Herb I was a dry sponge waiting to soak it all up; and there he was. And I soaked it all up."

■ He stayed with Lubalin for six years and then, feeling his oats, started his own firm, Alan Peckolick Graphic Design. "Herb and I had a very strange relationship; when we first met and he offered me that job and I

Lubalin, Smith, Carnese & Peckolick logo, 1976–1978.

was just an immature kid from Queens (my family had moved from the Bronx by then), I set him up and put him on a pedestal… for weeks he would say, 'Stop calling me Mr. Lubalin; call me Herb.' I grew in maturity and grew as a designer: I began to push back at Herb and wouldn't take everything he suggested as gospel; we had some raging fights about design. I was already doing a lot of freelance work; mostly book jackets, and I thought I could do it without Herb. When I left to start Alan Peckolick Graphic Design is when the friendship started."

■ In 1976, Peckolick returned to join Lubalin as a Vice President and Creative Director. At the time, the firm was called Lubalin Smith Carnese (Lubalin's partners were Ernie Smith and Tom Carnese). Not long after, the name was changed to LSC&P. Peckolick's designs were winning every award in the business, but, he says, "My success surprised me. I was petrified by my own success. Of course I loved winning awards, but

For the anniversary of the renamed firm, the Boston Art Directors Club designed a poster celebrating the new addition.

Lubalin Peckolick logo, 1978–1981.

I just didn't understand what it all meant. When I thought of all the honors I'd gotten, I just thought, 'Thank God I have a job and I love to learn and I love what I'm doing.' Because of the awards I was in demand as a speaker, but this was so difficult for me that I would start throwing up three days in advance."

■ In 1978, Lubalin started to cut back on his work in the office when he became ill with cancer, and Peckolick ran the company for three years; in 1981, Herb Lubalin died. "I became his heir apparent. I loved Herb and I owe everything to Herb, no doubt about it. And I miss him still."

■ A series of moves, recombinations, and rebirths of the firm ensued over the next several years. In 1983, Peckolick took the staff and clients and formed a new corporation with Seymour Chwast at Pushpin Studios, which was then renamed Pushpin Lubalin Peckolick.

From 1983 to 1986, Alan partnered with Seymour Chwast at Pushpin Lubalin Peckolick.

PeckolickInc.

Peckolick Inc. logo, 1986.

■ In 1987, Alan left to start Peckolick + Partners with a company that had been a major client, Corporate Annual Reports. They set him up with an office and staff in their company and they owned a piece of it. Peckolick pitched General Motors and AT&T and got both accounts; other major clients came in because of those two.

■ Corporate Annual Reports was subsequently bought out by the British design firm Addison, and Peckolick soon became a part of a multi-national design firm based in London. "They did not want Peckolick + Partners but they wanted me as creative director."

■ In 1993, he decided to start his own company (Peckolick Design Consultants) and moved into his wife's design office (Jessica Weber Design, Inc.). "I had annual report work that I continued, and I consulted with Jessica, which

Peckolick + Partners, 1987.

was a lot more pleasant than chasing down new clients. But I was going into a midlife crisis and starting to let the business slide. I really didn't like going out and getting the work—despite the successes with GM and AT&T, I was never really good at networking. I liked being a designer, doing the aesthetics. I wasn't a particularly good businessman, or a rainmaker. A backroom guy is what I should have always been."

■ "The problem with my career was that you go off on a creative adventure and after a few years you win awards and people are writing about you. Then you get older and more senior and you are meeting with clients more of the time and overseeing young designers, doing less and less design. That's the nature of the business…the better it got, the worse it got."

■ "By 1995, I found myself bored and restless; ready for a new chapter to open in my life. This ennui lasted for several years, until I had an epiphany; one day I took the afternoon off and went to the movies, which I had never done before. After leaving the theater, I passed an art supply store; I walked in and decided to buy some paints and brushes... and I went home and started painting. I had never painted; literally had never held a paintbrush in my hand...I found the process challenging but satisfying. After a while I realized that I always loved drawing letters; I could still draw a rough so tight that people would think it was finished. And all the years that I had been traveling I had always taken photographs of walls and signs... so the first real painting I did was of a wall in France with an ad for the aperitif Dubonnet. When I started to paint, I pulled out that picture and worked on it for about two weeks. When I finished, there was something about it that bothered me. I asked Jessica what she thought. 'Sure there's something wrong. You corrected all the letter spacing on a century-old sign.' Now that I am a more seasoned painter, I use my photographs for a particular architec-

"After 40 years in the business, mistake possible—and a

tural element and then I put them away and add my own things. A friend told me that he liked my paintings and that he had a friend who had a gallery. One thing led to another and now I have had many shows, and this has become my new life."

■ Peckolick's painting career has in fact become a direct outgrowth of his graphic design career. (He still accepts design assignments that he finds of interest.) His painting is motivated and informed by his attachment to letterforms, specifically letterforms he has "discovered" in his photography: signage from worn building surfaces, signage ravaged by time and urban wear-and-tear, signage that has been revealed when buildings are torn down. Peckolick weaves these "ghosts" of civilizations past into his own compositions; his paintings have detailed, photo-realistic surfaces that require tight control of his medium. He brings a weariness and humanity to the

I have made every bloody few I created myself"

portrayal of these often-overlooked remnants of urban activity; this speaks to his own deep identification with his subject, a subject that has fascinated him since his earliest days at Pratt Institute. (How ironic is it that Peckolick was once spurned by Pratt's illustration department, now that he has distinguished himself as an artist?) Since 2000, Peckolick's paintings have been exhibited in both the United States and abroad.

■ When asked about his design philosophy, Peckolick muses, "I have a very simple one: solving my clients' problems in the most aesthetically pleasing way—period! Type is the format I go to first. Some designers go to a photograph or an illustration first. But for me it has always been type. That's how I was trained by Herb. I look back on my career and I still can't believe the incredibly rich friendships and experiences it has afforded me. I am a very lucky guy!"—**Ina Saltz**

Alan in 2012.

BERLIN

IN AUGUST 1981, ERICH HONECKER ORDERED THE BLOCKING OFF OF EAST BERLIN FROM WEST BERLIN BY MEANS OF BARBED WIRE AND ANTITANK OBSTACLES. STREETS WERE TORN UP, AND BARRICADES OF PAVING STONES WERE ERECTED. PEOPLE LIVING IN EAST BERLIN AND THE GERMAN DEMOCRATIC REPUBLIC WERE NO LONGER ALLOWED TO ENTER WEST BERLIN. THIS INCLUDED 60,000 WHO HAD BEEN WORKING IN THE CITY.

THE WALL WAS 166 KM LONG, CUT THROUGH 192 STREETS, 97 OF THEM LEADING TO EAST BERLIN AND 95 INTO EAST GERMANY. THE BERLIN WALL WAS HEAVILY GUARDED AND AROUND A HUNDRED PEOPLE WERE KILLED.

WITH THE COLLAPSE OF COMMUNISM IN 1989 THE BERLIN WALL WAS REMOVED AND THE TWO GERMAN REPUBLICS WERE UNITED.

ABOVE AND OPPOSITE
I visited Berlin as a tourist several years ago. The Berliners had left remnants of the Wall in empty paths all over the city, snaking from East to West. A few years later, a design organization I belong to was having its annual meeting there. Members were asked to contribute a poster on any aspect of the city. It was an easy solution for me. I was so moved by my experience from my first visit that I felt compelled to create a painting from the poster, as well. Our parrot, Walter, served as my critic.

ORDERED THE BLOCKING OFF
CIGARETTES
JOB
TOURISTEN-KAFFEE
GRAPHIC DESIGN IN JAPAN 5
a good

1. TYPO-GRAPH SPEAKING

For all its communicative value, a piece of typography can still lay on a page like a "lox." Or it can sing and dance. It's all in the hands of the designer.

Good type serves as both the message and the aesthetic. I give words their own language by designing letters that graphically suggest meaning. They impact the viewer on a subconscious level. When designing anything, I start by reading the copy first, to get the essence of the message that needs to be conveyed. Then I look

ICALLY

for graphic opportunities. This is when the creative juices start to flow. As a designer, not only do I make type talk, but I give it a mood—and sometimes a temper. It can be violent or peaceful, irreverent or polite, severe or whimsical. This is what expressive typography is all about.

Sometimes I can't believe I'm the same person who in art school thought typography was just the stuff that screwed up my designs. My mentor and revolutionary graphic designer, Herb Lubalin, always said, "The best type never gets noticed." I added: "Unless you want it to."

BEARDS

Reginald Reynolds

The fascinating history of beards through the ages.
"First-rate entertainment." —San Francisco Chronicle

OPPOSITE AND RIGHT These two book jackets succeeded in very different ways. Both involved facial hair. In *Beards*, the title lettering supports my philosophy of letting type talk. In *The Bedside Book of Bastards*, I used a villain's mustache to illustrate the point.

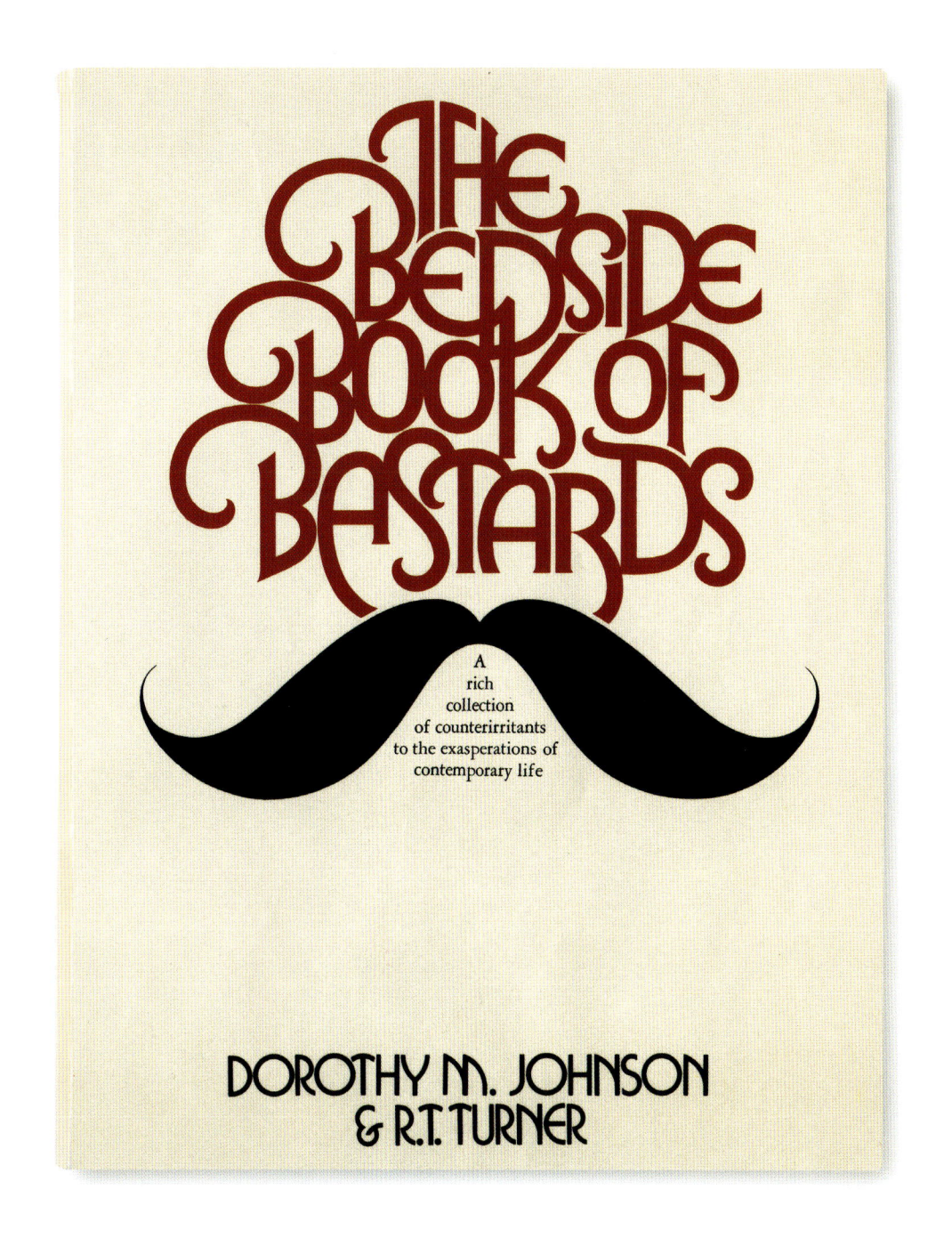

ishing you an

ncomplicated 1982.

LEFT AND BELOW
We were lucky at our firm to have Tony DiSpigna with us. He was, and still is, one of the world's preeminent letterform designers. I wanted to design our holiday greeting card with pure, elegant pieces of typography. Spencerian script is one of the most beautiful ways words can be written. I gave Tony a very rough tissue of my ideas, and he transformed them into pieces of magic. When you look closely at the enlargements of the letter "W," you can see the genius of Tony's hand.

LEFT AND BELOW
I had very serious reservations about the potential success of *The Nothing Book*. My client wanted to create a hardcover book with completely blank pages, as a tongue-in-cheek bow to the memo pad. When it sold over half a million copies in the first year, and my cover was seen all over the world, I had to admit he was right. This certainly improves on the adage "less is more."

THE NOTHING BOOK.

Wanna Make Something Of It?

For: poets, cooks, travelers, writers, diarists, students, comedians, brides, grandparents, decorators, kids, tourists, doodlers, secretaries, list-makers, forgetters, artists, sketchers, businesswomen, businessmen, leaf-pressers, gift-givers, minimalists, and all of us who've ever wanted to do a book.

LEFT, BELOW LEFT, AND BELOW
Good-bye to All That was an homage to the art of cigarette smoking. I used iconic movie stills as the medium. Think of all the classic movie scenes with W.C. Fields, Bette Davis, Paul Henreid, Humphrey Bogart, and Lauren Bacall, and you'll get the idea. The cover was a riff on the old Lucky Strike Cigarettes tin from the 1940s.

OPPOSITE
Every once in a while, you are handed a job where you can simply have fun. As the title of this catalog for the Neenah Paper Company suggests, I was given the task of introducing a new line of writing paper. In doing so, I showcased the influence of historical schools of art on modern design. Taking samples from my own portfolio and juxtaposing them against work from different eras, I demonstrated how various movements throughout time are translated into a personal aesthetic.

DESIGN INFLUENCES ON NEENAH CLASSIC

LAID & CLASSIC® LINEN

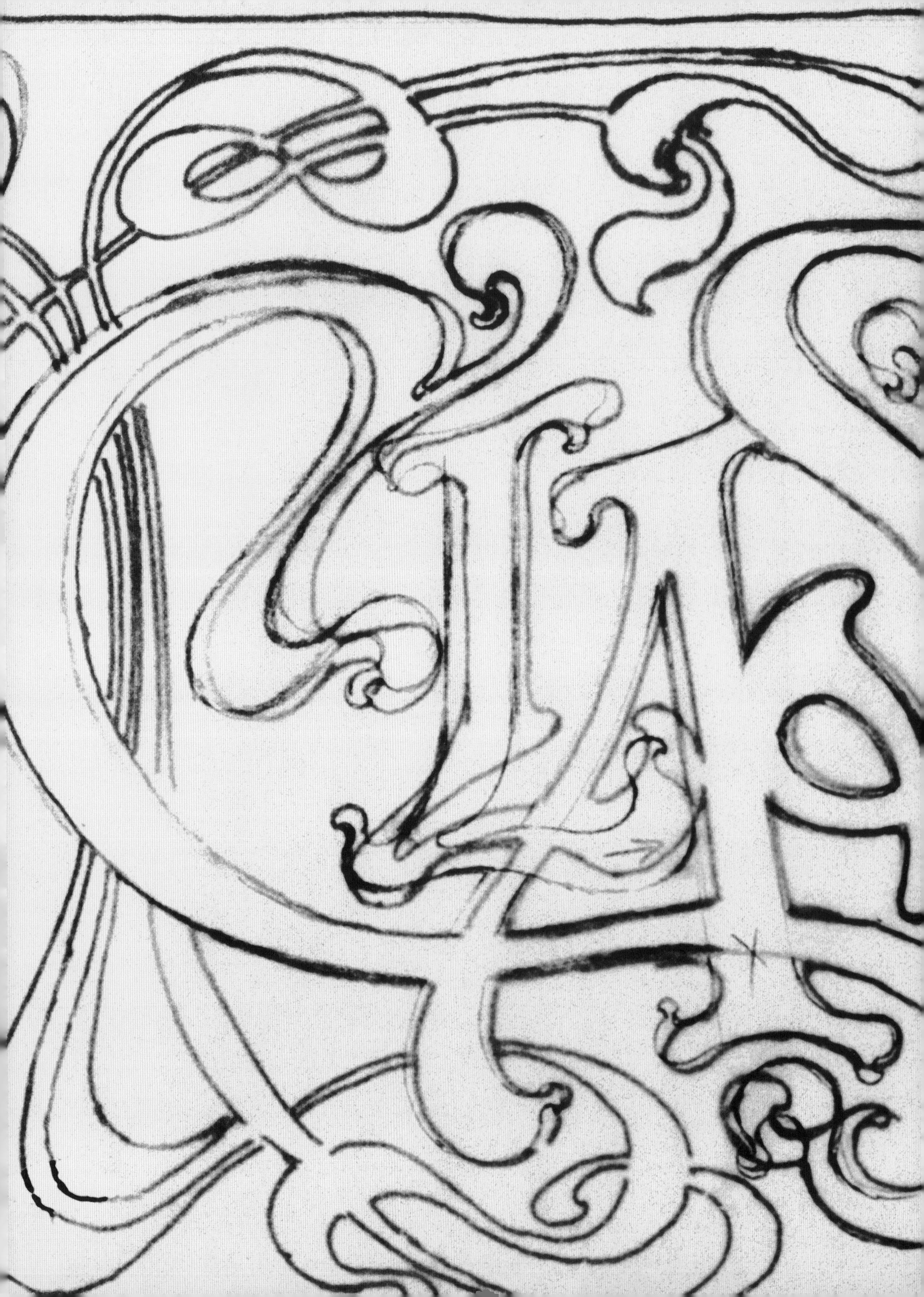

Hand-drawn lettering has come back into fashion over the past decade. While there are many amazing letterers and typographers working today, to my eye, there will never be anything to match exceptional hand-lettering. We take it for granted how quickly we can change a line or a design digitally. While the computer offers amazing options for new possibilities, it also abandons certain aspects of a well-conceived piece of type created by hand. The level of concentration needed by both the designer and the letterer—knowing that they will have to start from the beginning if the design doesn't work—brings a sense of both excitement and pressure. Examples on the overleaf prove my point.

OVERLEAF
I sketched out dozens of versions of the cover design. The one I decided to use is shown with its Pantone breakdown and a subtle note from master letterer Tony DiSpigna.

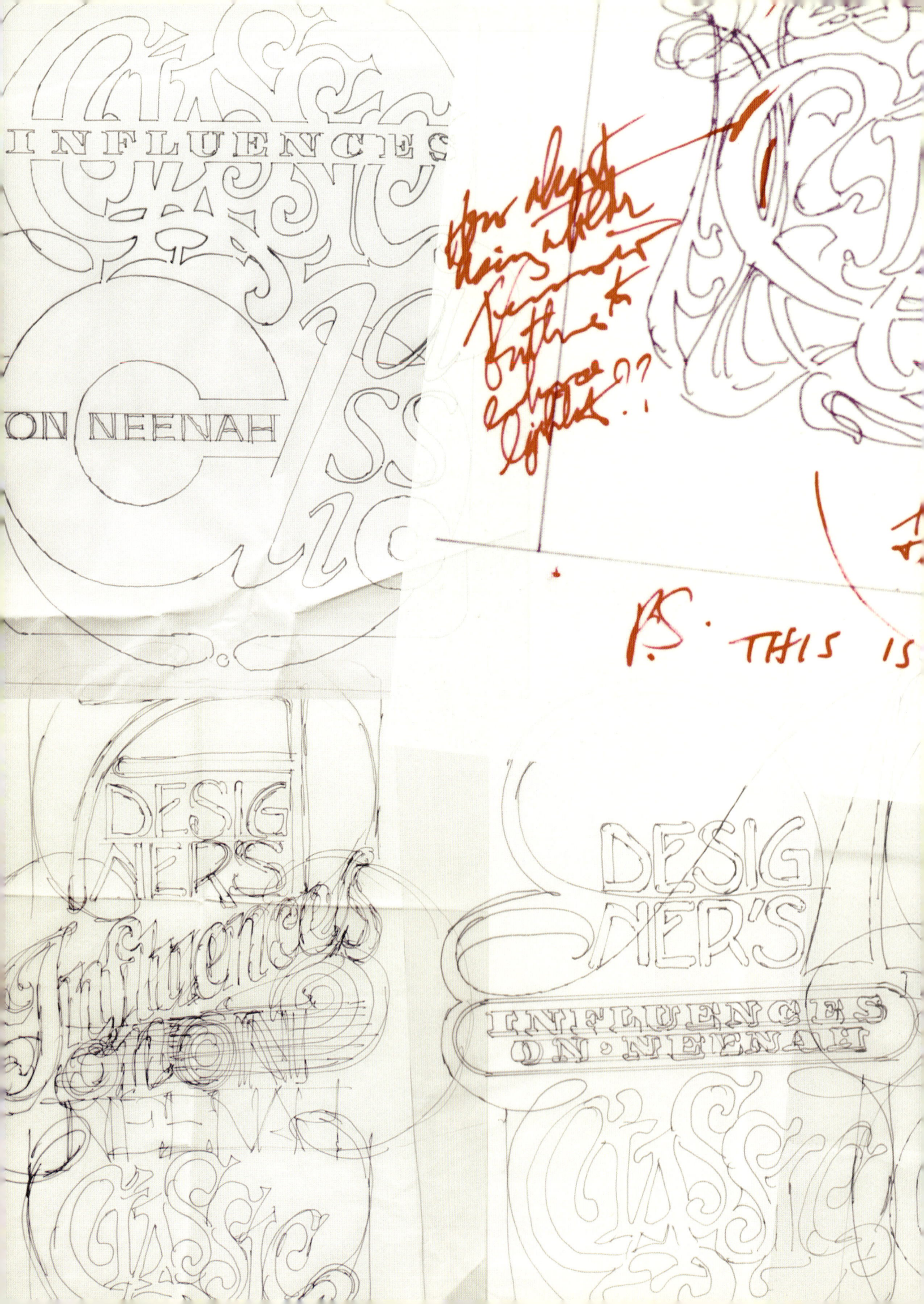

INFLUENCES
ON NEENAH

P.S. THIS IS

DESIGNERS
Influences

DESIGNER'S
INFLUENCES
ON·NEENAH

A REAL BITCH!

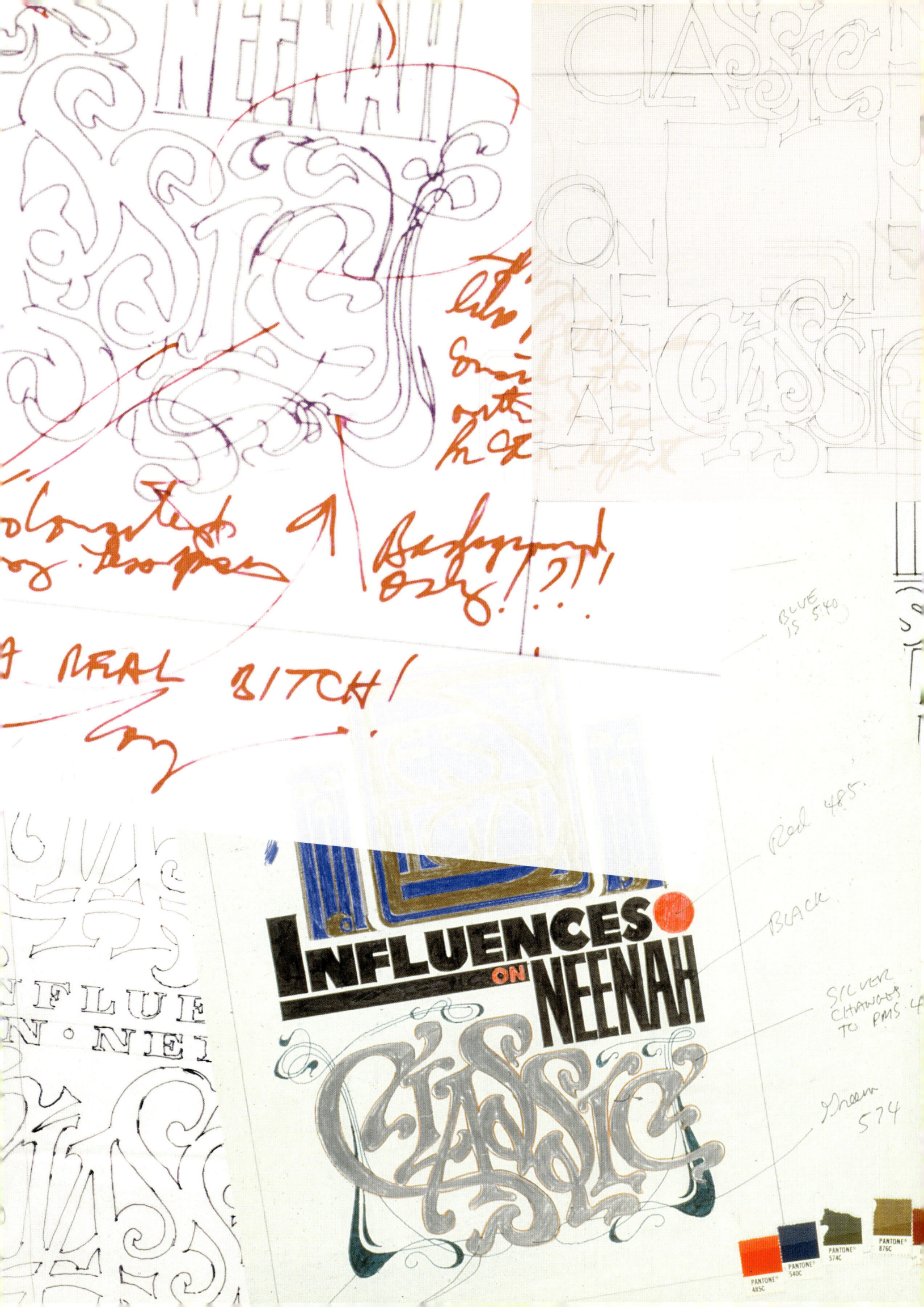

INFLUENCES ON NEENAH CLASSIC

BELOW The logo in blue is one I created for a European banking group. It was in the Wiener Werkstätte design movement that I found my inspiration.

SOCIETE GENERALE IS ONE OF THE LARGEST BANKING CHAINS IN FRANCE. WHEN THEY DECIDED TO UPDATE THEIR EXISTING LOGO, THEY ASKED FOR A SYMBOL THAT WOULD SALUTE THEIR EUROPEAN HERITAGE OF SWISS GRAPHICS. THE INTERLOCKING LETTERFORMS CREATE A MARK THAT IS REALLY MORE THAN THE SUM OF ITS LETTER FORMS AND A UNIQUE SOLUTION FOR SOCIETE GENERALE. RATHER THAN BEING AN ABSTRACT DESIGN, THE LIGATURE OF LETTERFORMS PERSONALIZES THE IDENTITY—LIKE A THUMB PRINT OR SIGNATURE—AND EVOKES THE FLAT SHAPES AND CLEAN, LEGIBLE STYLE OF THE WIENER WERKSTÄTTE.

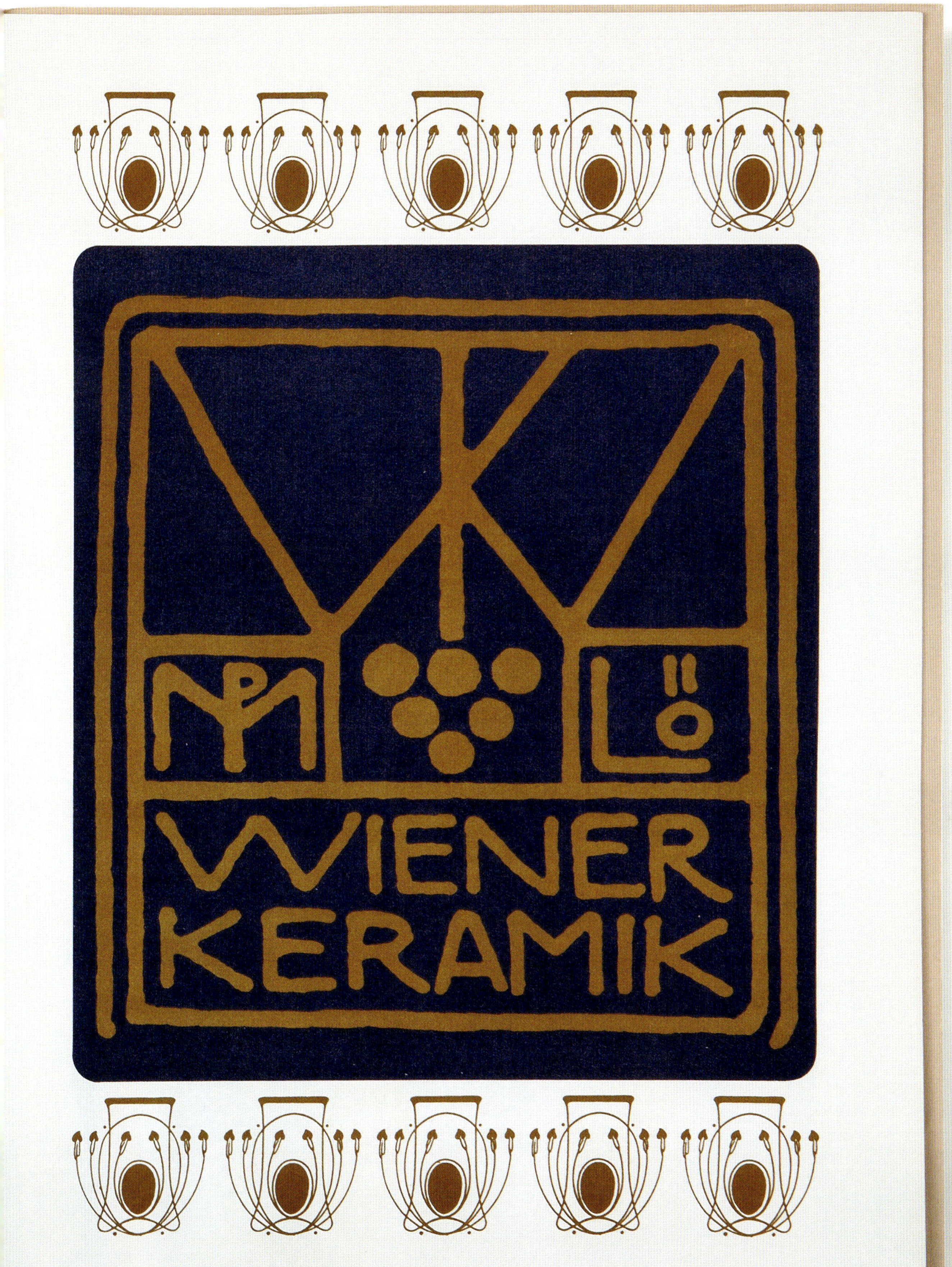
WIENER
KERAMIK

BELOW My love of vintage sports cars helped me create the "retro" branding the client needed to support the name of his new product.

The diner I remember from my youth was a thing of streamlined beauty. The sides glimmered with fluted stainless steel and a neon sign illuminated the top. It was the place to be.... Where you would show off your hot rod and check out the girls. And we went there when ever we could... after sock hops, after football games, after class... because it was cool and that's where it was happening.

Since then, the diner has developed a powerful national mystique. We see it today in nostalgic movies and the sudden popularity of the-diner-as-gourmet-dining-experience around the country.

For this new soft drink, American POP, I recreated the aura of the diner. The letterforms suggest its neon signature. And the silver foil label shines like the buffed and polished chrome of the decade's finest "muscle machines."

The coloring of the labels is also significant. American POP comes in six flavors, yet the beverage itself is always quite clear. The silver foil labels with their individual spots of color communicate the beverage flavors and become a dynamic color coding system... giving American POP a sophisticated, recognizable presence on the grocery shelf.

11

CLASSIC® Laid Text, Pageant Rose, 80 lb.

BELOW For many years, I collected Art Nouveau posters. The Helena Rubinstein Company asked me to explore a new direction for their branding. I turned to

Alphonse Mucha. Although the company decided to stay with their existing logo, this remains one of my favorites.

Helena Rubinstein

I try to imbue each logo or identity I create with the unique corporate personality of my client. I'm not interested in designing an abstract symbol or forcing a company to mold itself to my design. I strive to create a logo that's warm, that people can relate to.

Everything about Helena Rubinstein — the company, its products and personality — is feminine, beautiful or beautifying. The influence of Art Nouveau and Alphonse Mucha (whose work I greatly admire and collect) on this identity is unmistakable. And, I think, quite fitting. The logo has a formal, calligraphic quality; yet, is still sensuous and feminine. It has a stately feeling, almost heraldic — like the royal monogram on a Faberge egg.

Zeitung

LEFT
Zeitung means newspaper in German. I was asked to create this mark to be used on the masthead.

BELOW
In Greek mythology, the phoenix rises from the ashes. My client, Phoenix House, helped drug addicts overcome their addictions and rise up again. This logo really designed itself for me.

WHO IS? WISE
ONE WHO LEARNS FROM ALL PEOPLE.

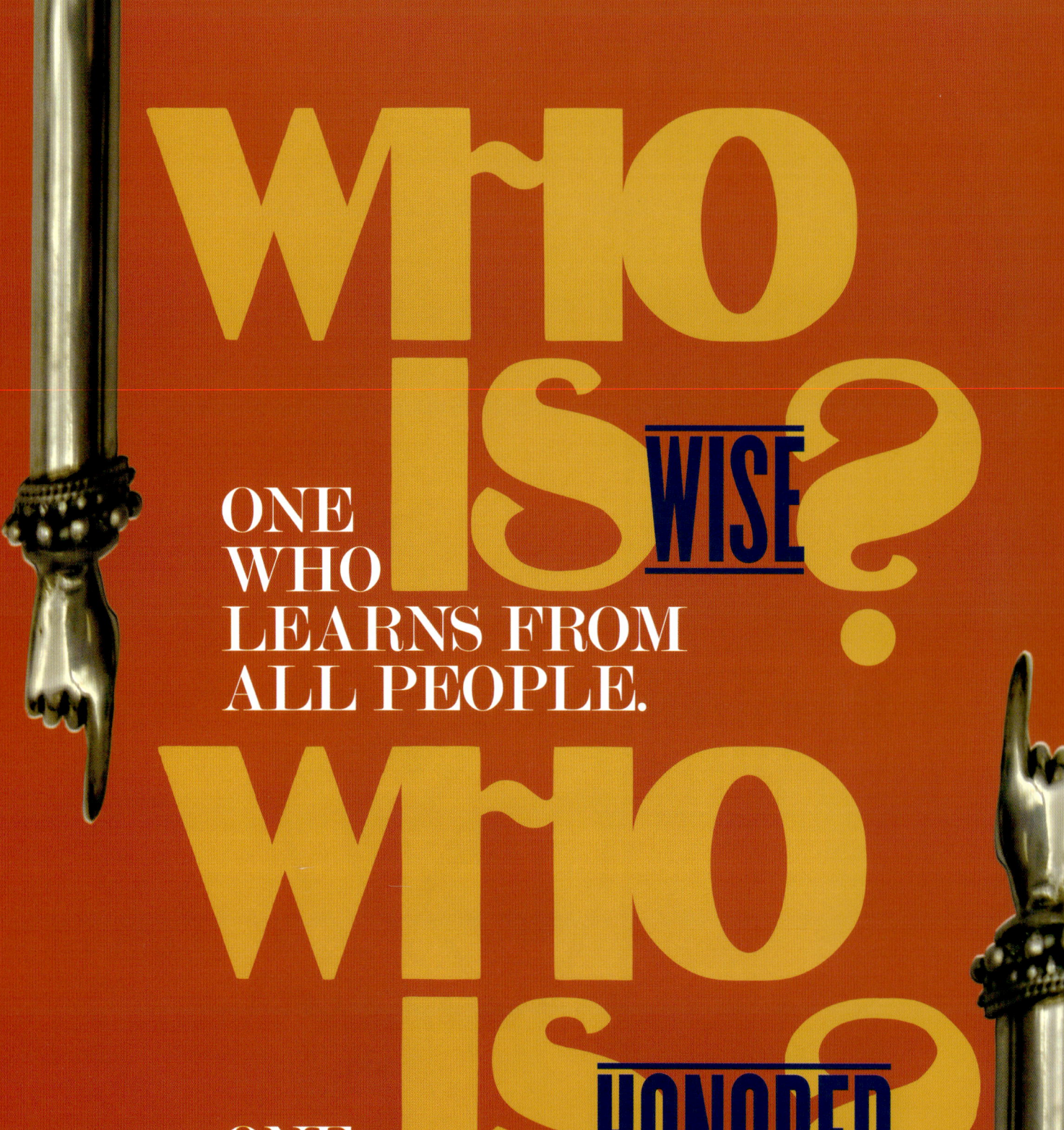

WHO IS? HONORED
ONE WHO HONORS EVERYONE.

BEN-ZOMA, PIRKE AVOT 4:1

OPPOSITE
From 1950 to 1975, the Container Corporation of America commissioned designers and artists to participate in the now-famous poster series, Great Ideas of Western Man. In 2012, the Harold Grinspoon Foundation asked 18 designers to create a series entitled "Visions and Voices," devoted to great Jewish ideas. We were asked to choose from a selection of quotes. In my solution, I felt an illustrative element was necessary to making the poster look immediately "Jewish." The silver, pointed finger—a *yad*—is a pointer used when reading the Torah.

RIGHT
The Center for Jewish History's mark was also to be used as building signage. It was to be discreet and elegant, and I wanted it to be vertical. Hand-lettering was the only solution. Every letter was hand-drawn to create custom ligatures and combinations to form a perfect square. My letterforms were based on classic Roman letters.

Eleven One
Ten Two
Nine Three
Eight Four
Seven Five
Six

THESE PAGES
Often, clients ask me to help them name their products. In this case, I not only designed the exterior signage for my client but also named it. Paper & Ink was a shop that sold only paper products. Tucked away in a plaza a few steps below street level, it was easy to miss. I created a kiosk that rose above the street level to announce its presence. I designed the name to look like a ribbon. I couldn't resist adding a working clock to draw attention from passersby. Of course, the Roman numerals were represented in Spencerian script.

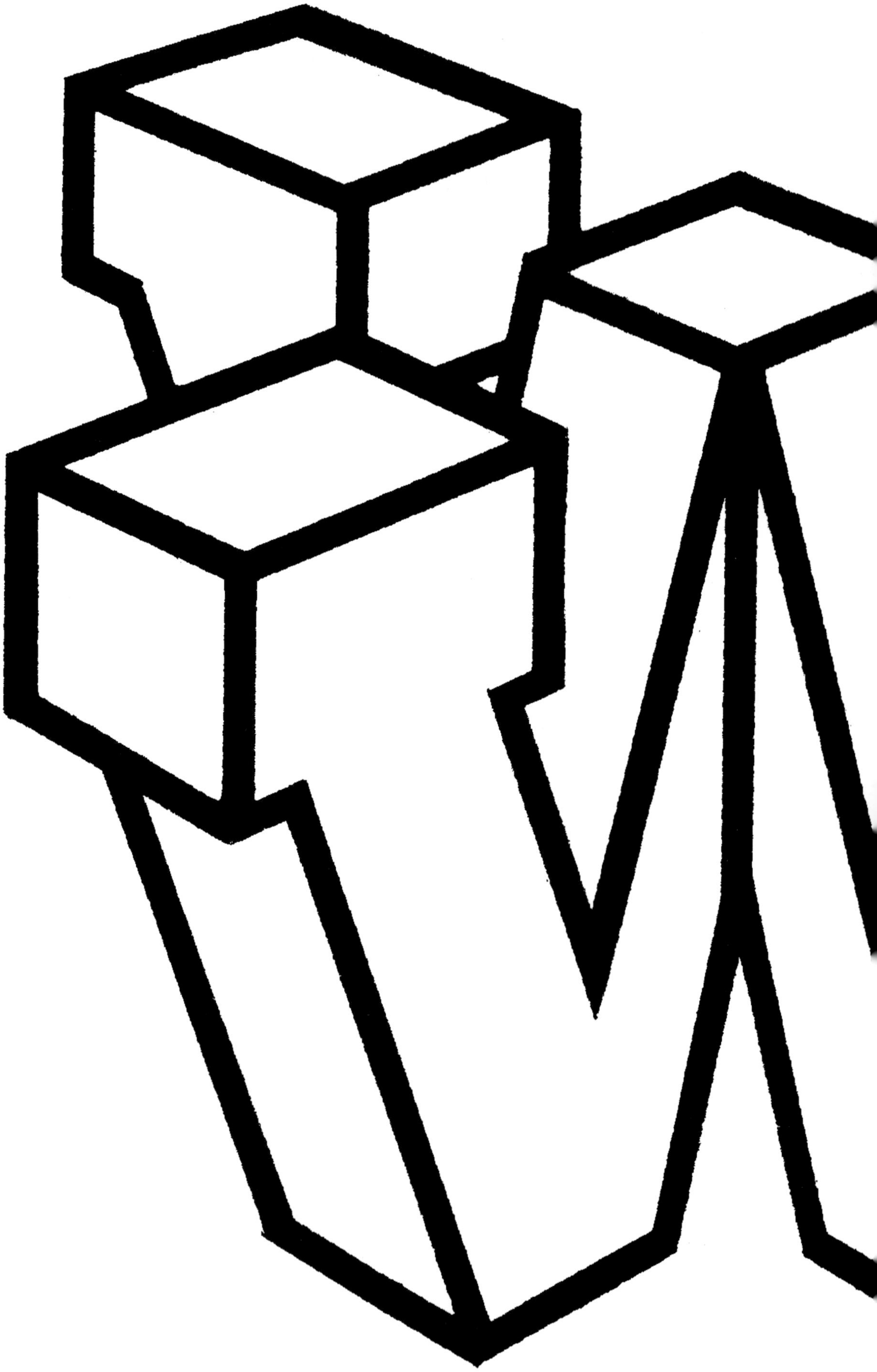

LEFT
Woodpecker products designed modular furniture. I turned the "W" into the base of a heavy modular table. Sometimes a client's products lead me to a solution more easily than others.

BELOW
One of those cases where the client's business did not lead me to an easy solution, the Wisconsin (another "W") Dairy Council oversees statewide dairy nutrition education. This was a difficult assignment. I got hooked on milk drops after trying dozens of other directions. Also, I knew they were expecting a corporate, abstract mark, not a typographic one. I created an organic sun-shape by repeating white teardrops that hopefully resembled milk. They loved it.

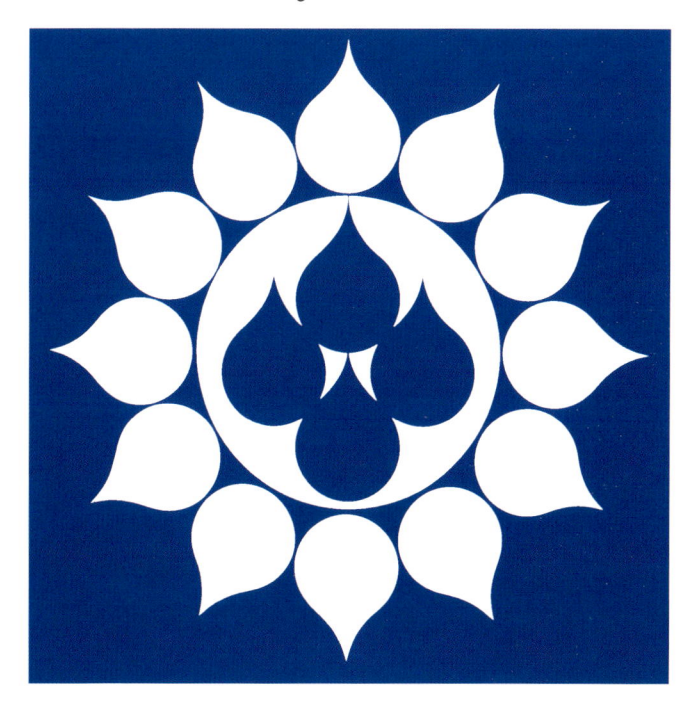

LEFT
As soon as I opened my own studio after leaving Herb Lubalin, Inc., I created a brochure with samples of my work. The ad, which I placed in trade magazines, announced the availability of "The Peckolick Papers."

OPPOSITE
I was asked to speak at a typographic design conference in Texas and designed this promotional for myself. For a guy who can't spell, I somehow managed to pull off the design of a completely alliterative poster.

OVERLEAF LEFT
Designers sometimes joke they'll go to the mat to defend a concept. I was honored to be asked to design all the graphics for the annual show of the New York Art Directors Club. The theme that year was "commitment." The concept came to me like a bolt of lightning. The master stroke was provided by Kinuko Y. Craft's painting.

OVERLEAF RIGHT
Designing the cover of the ninth annual for the New York Type Directors Club was a daunting task. The annual is kept and used as a reference. I wanted to bring a sense of history and gravitas to honor the project. I went back to basics. The Roman alphabet has a definitive structure. In my library, I found a book about the creation of Roman letterforms and their architecture. I used this as my cover inspiration.

ALAN PECKOLICK

PECKOLICK
+**P**ARTNERS'
PRESIDENT
PROUDLY
PRESENTS
PROJECTS
PRODUCED
PRIOR TO
PECKOLICK
+**P**ARTNERS,
PLUS
PROJECTS
PRODUCED BY
PECKOLICK
+**P**ARTNERS.
PERTINENT QUESTIONS
PERTAINING TO
PECKOLICK OR
PREVIOUSLY MENTIONED
PERIODS OR
PROJECTS
POLITELY ADDRESSED
PERIOD!

COMMITMENT

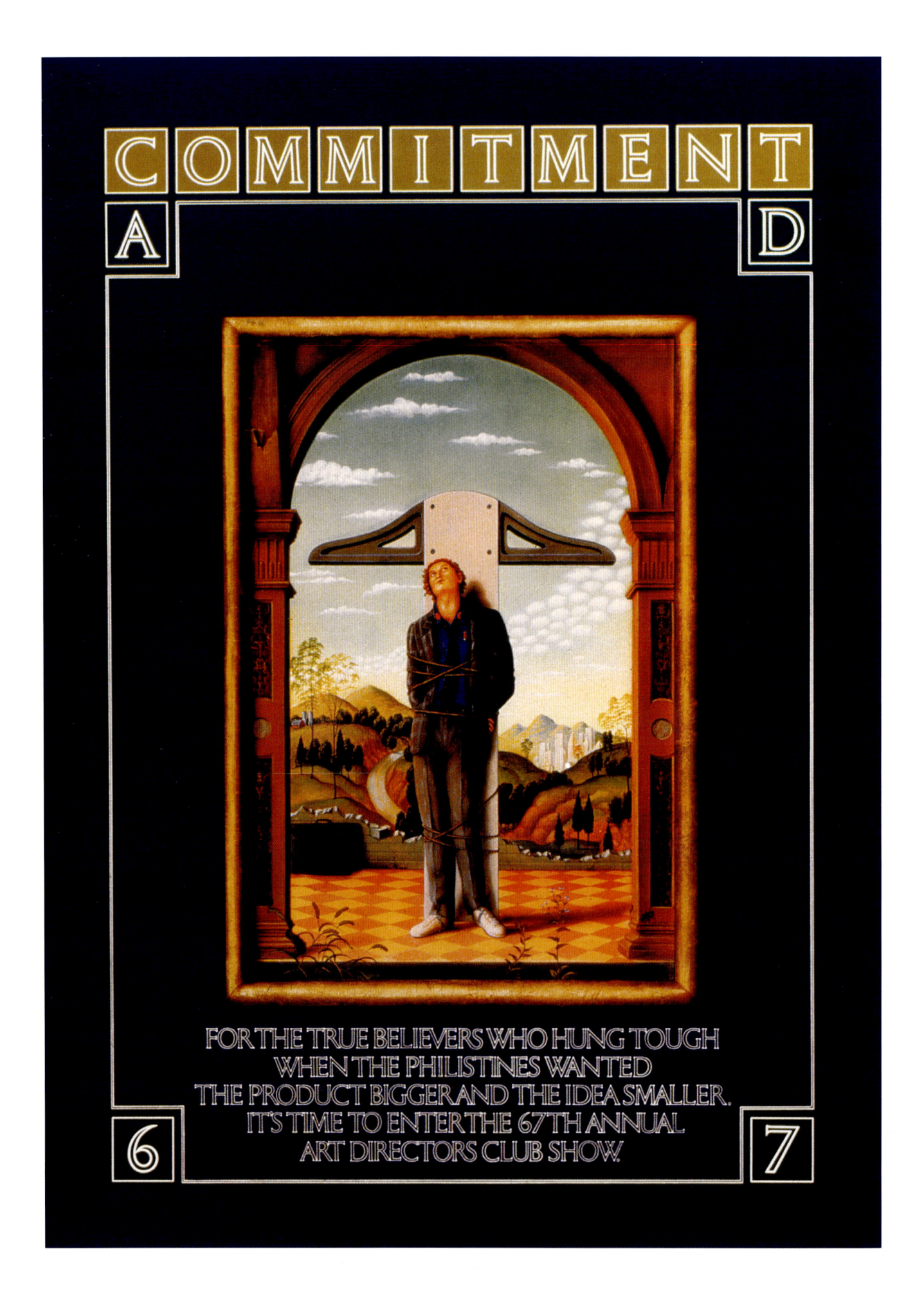

A D

6 7

FOR THE TRUE BELIEVERS WHO HUNG TOUGH
WHEN THE PHILISTINES WANTED
THE PRODUCT BIGGER AND THE IDEA SMALLER.
IT'S TIME TO ENTER THE 67TH ANNUAL
ART DIRECTORS CLUB SHOW.

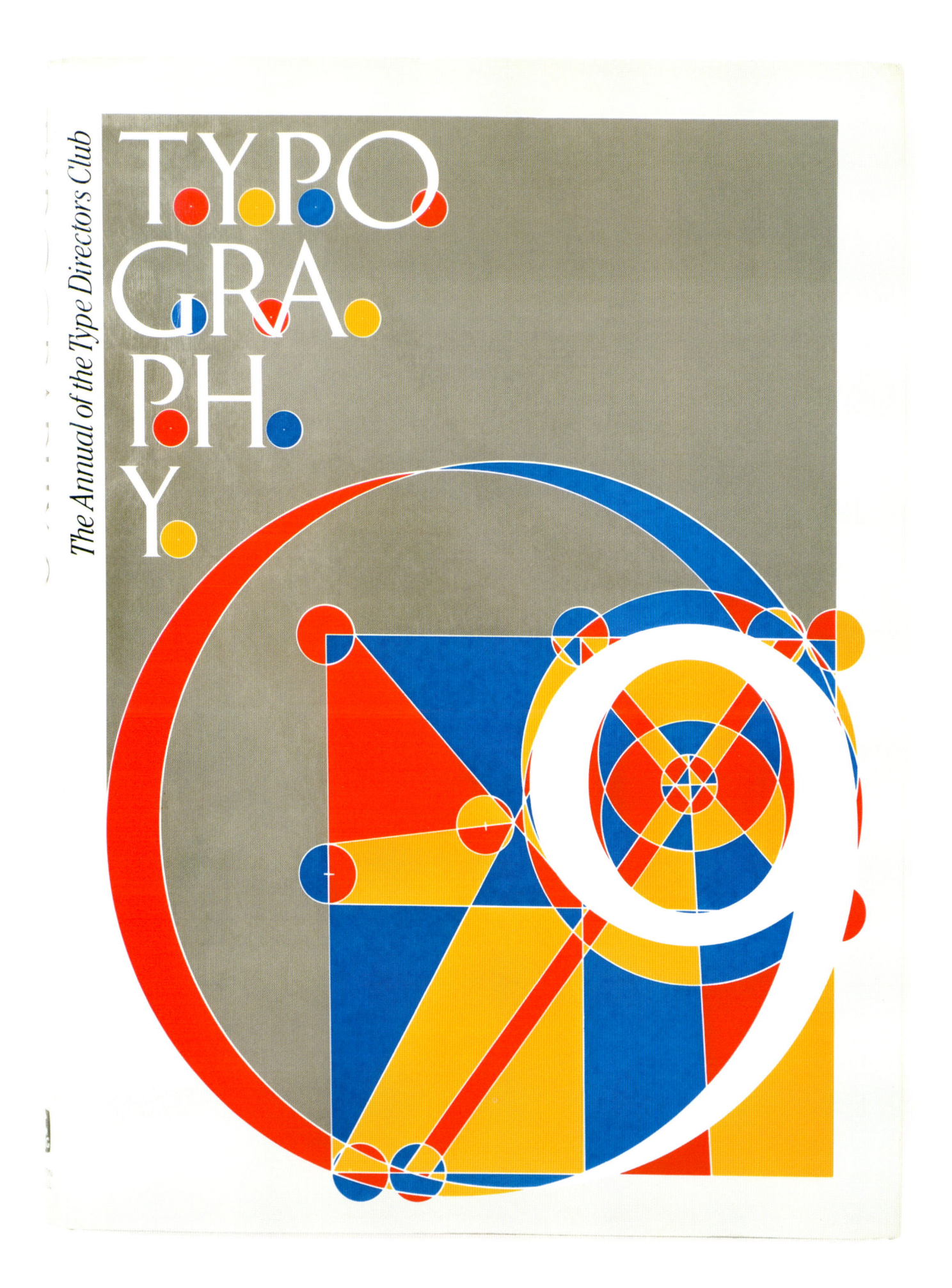

TYPO
GRA
PH.
Y.

The Annual of the Type Directors Club

C O N N E C T I O N S

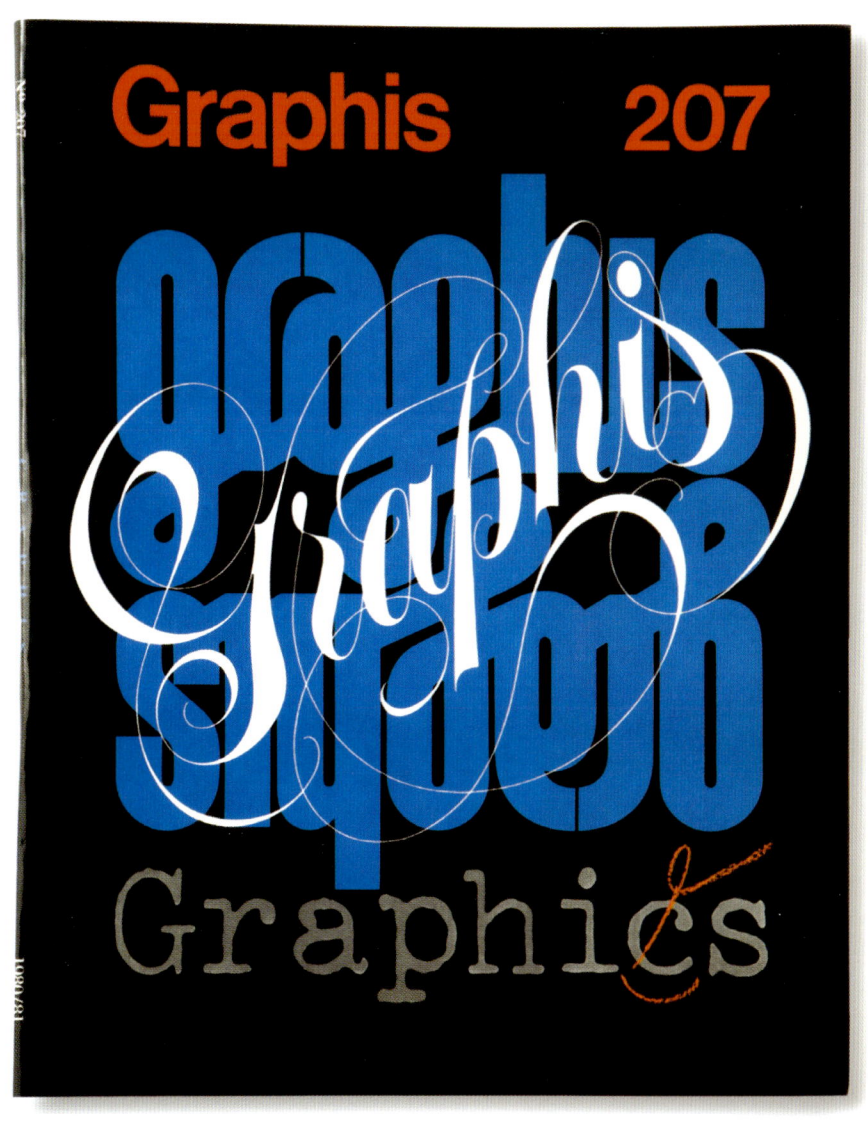

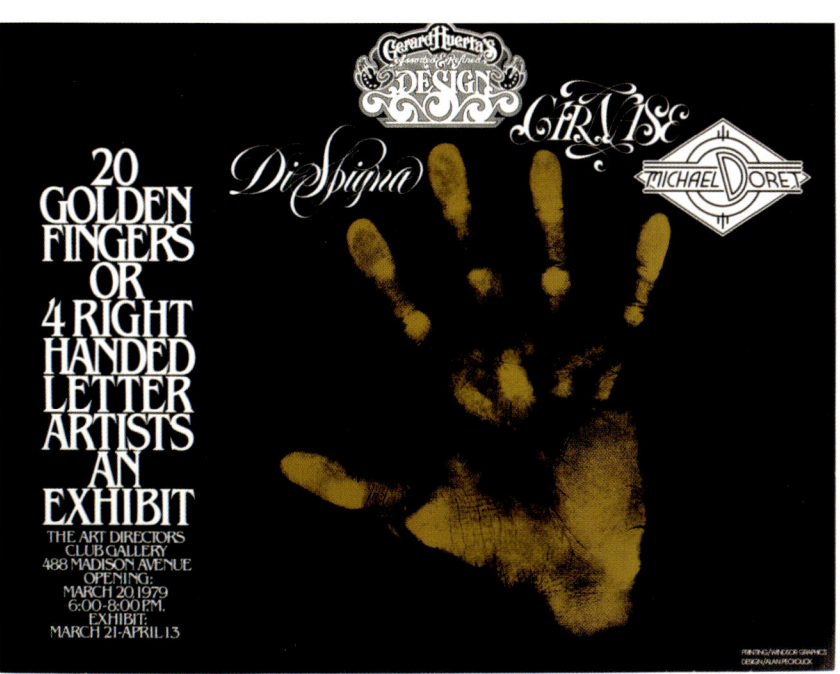

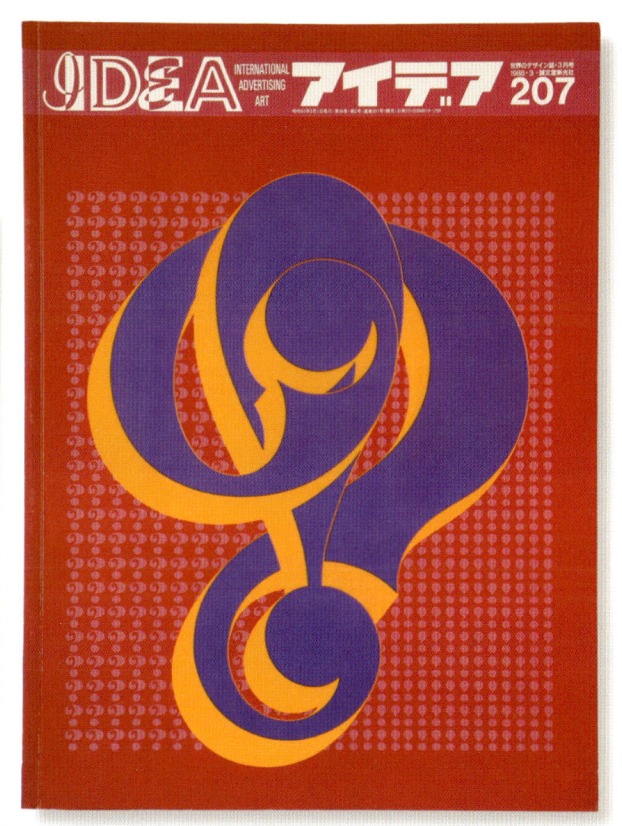

OPPOSITE
Neenah Paper asked a select group of graphic designers to interpret the word "connections." In my world of letterform design, there is nothing greater than the ampersand. Throughout history, it has been used to connect great thoughts and great words. So, I married two of them.

ABOVE
As designers, we are asked to solve problems (the question mark) and come up with solutions (the exclamation point). Combining the two, I created an interrobang—a non-standard punctuation mark—for the cover of the Japanese design magazine *Idea*.

ABOVE LEFT
Graphis wrote an article on the associates of Herb Lubalin, Inc.—there were just three of us at the time. The cover was a collaborative effort, with each of us designing our own logo: I did the blue letters, Tony DiSpigna did the white, and Ernie Smith did the grey.

LEFT
I proposed an exhibit on hand-lettering to the New York Art Directors Club. They loved the idea. I named it and created the poster, which is self-explanatory.

There are many reasons why, and each one is as valid as the next, but inevitably type plays the supporting role to a lead image. Sometimes the immediate read of a photograph can put the reader right where you want them faster than elaborate twisting and turning of letterforms. But make no mistake, no matter how great the picture, it will not hide bad type. And no matter how solid the type, a photograph that misses the mark will bring down the whole page. The two elements need to work together, balancing each other for the sake of the clients' story.

LEFT AND OPPOSITE
These two covers were created for my Mexican client, Grupo Industrial Alfa. The graphic images were created to dominate; type was purposely put into a supporting role.

GRUPO INDUSTRIAL ALFA FINANCIAL STATEMENTS 1980

2. RADI-CAL ME

In today's culture of reality TV, YouTube videos, and internet tweets, there is little left that can still be considered shocking. Yet through all the visual overload, there is always room to twist, turn, or distort something to give it new meaning and attract the eye of your audience. The best designers know when to be tastefully vulgar or when to be boldly sophisticated. Yet walking the line between right and wrong—the *should we?* or *shouldn't we?*—is a monumental task, even in the hands of the experienced. The key is knowing which side of the line you want to be on, and how to convince others that they want to be there with you. Radical comes in all forms, whether it be turning to tradition when everyone else is looking away, leaping forward when everyone is creeping backward, or whispering when the world is screaming. It is a designer's job to make someone stop and take notice—whether they are seeing a piece in some digital form or, even more groundbreaking these days, actually holding it in their hands.

ABOVE AND RIGHT
When I first received the project to design the cover of a book on Rudolf Hess, Adolf Hitler's deputy in the Nazi movement, I knew immediately that I wanted to make the German cross, a strong symbol, very prominent. But I couldn't figure out how to fit it into the title. The answer presented itself when the cut-out letters, left on my desk, were accidentally turned at an angle. They fit together perfectly, like jigsaw puzzle pieces, and I had my cover.

The last of the Third Reich's imprisoned leaders and the truth behind his bizarre flight to Scotland

HESS

J. Bernard Hutton

The Progress of the Protestant

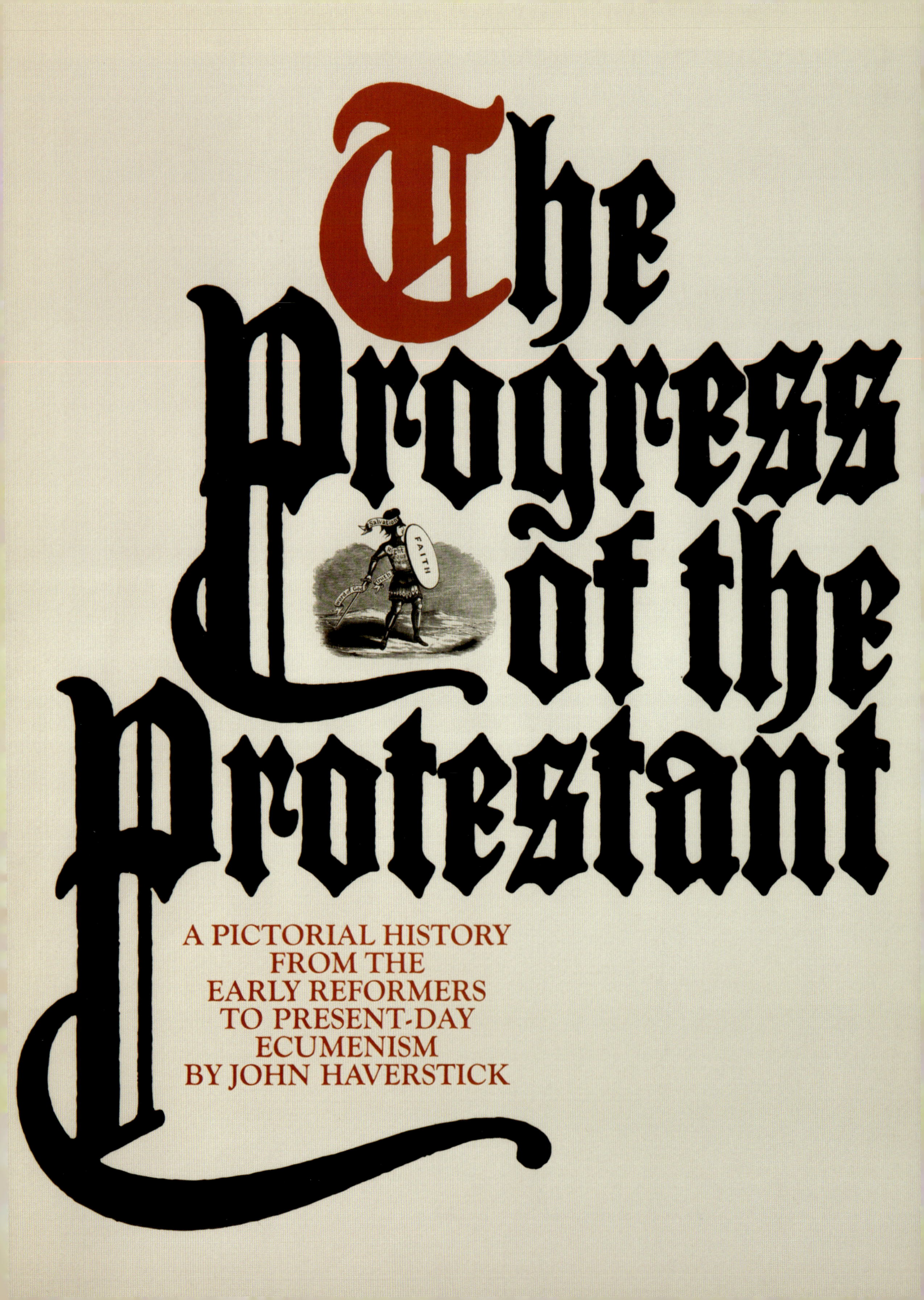

A PICTORIAL HISTORY
FROM THE
EARLY REFORMERS
TO PRESENT-DAY
ECUMENISM
BY JOHN HAVERSTICK

OPPOSITE
I have a vast collection of old type books in my reference library that I go to for constant inspiration. It helped in solving this book-jacket design. I found a wonderful wood type font, but as it lacked some of the letters I needed, I re-imagined what they might have looked like, and had them redrawn.

RIGHT
I positioned three horizontal type blocks and lined up the characters on the book jacket to suggest the flag used by Arab nationalists during the Arab revolution against the Ottoman Empire in World War I.

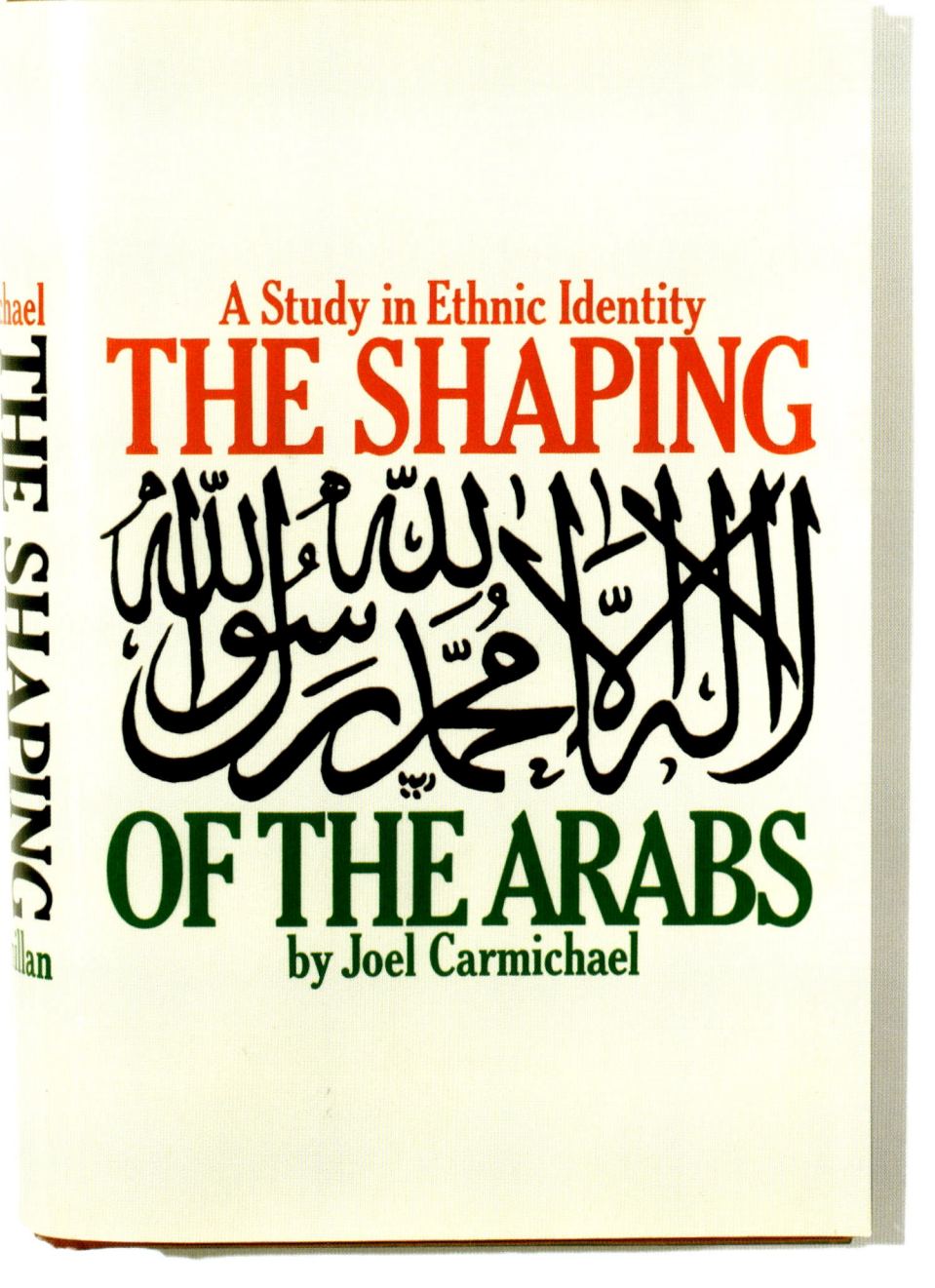

"GET THAT Nigger OFF THE FIELD!"

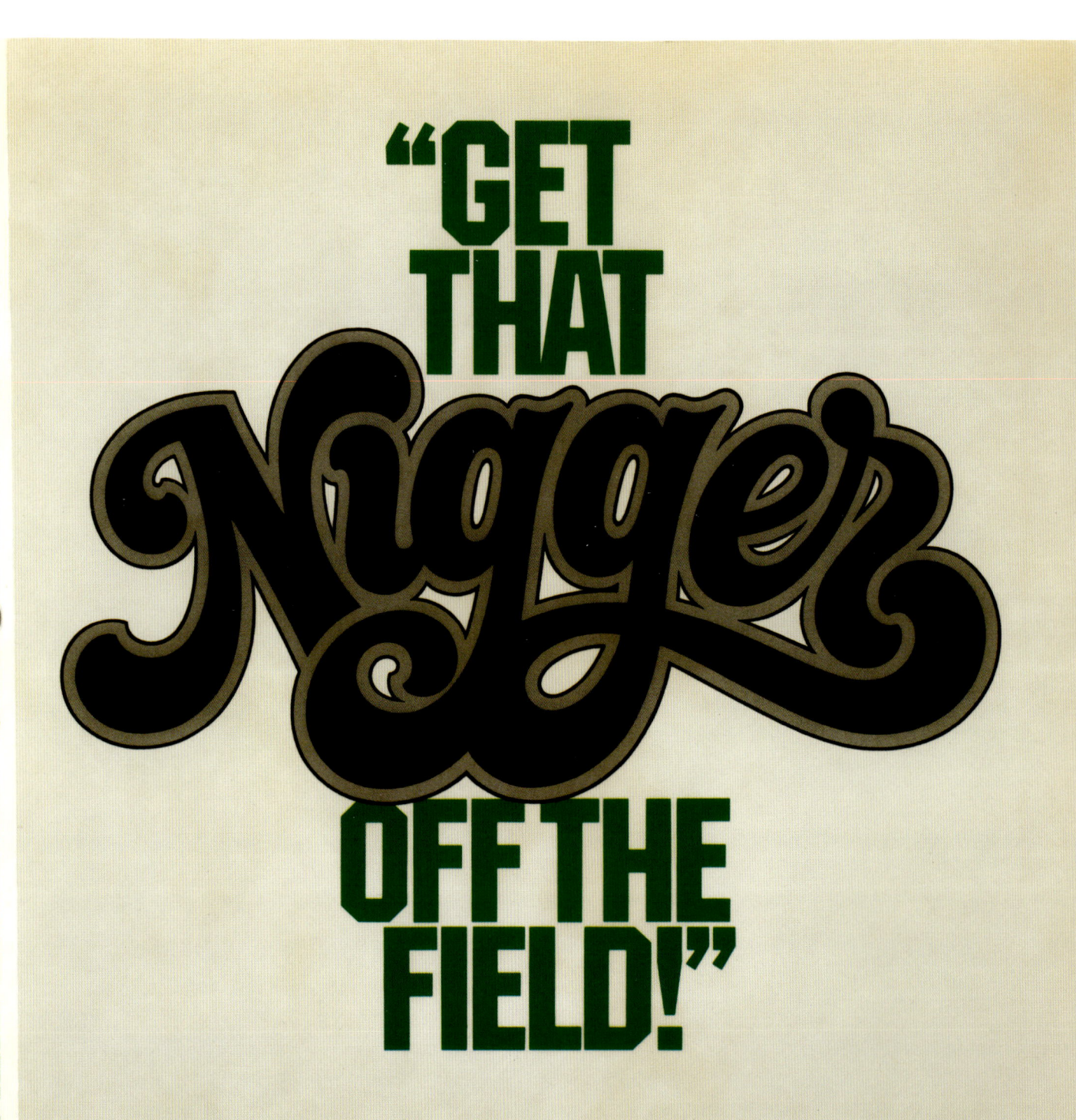

A Sparkling, Informal History of the Black Man in Baseball

ART RUST, JR.

OPPOSITE
At the time, the title of this book about the history of black American Baseball players was very shocking. Using the lettering style found on athletic uniforms, and accentuating the "N" word, the reader knew immediately what the book was all about.

BELOW
Marshall McLuhan was one of the most famous philosophers and thinkers of the 1950s. *Culture is Our Business* was one of his seminal books. The Hathaway Shirt Man campaign debuted in 1951 and was a creation of the Ogilvy & Mather advertising agency. The model wore an eye patch. This was so unique that the simple wearing of an eye patch became synonymous with Hathaway shirts. I chose this cultural phenomenon to use as my inspiration for the book jacket. What made the jacket really work was the black model we shot for the back cover who was identical, save for his race. And his tie.

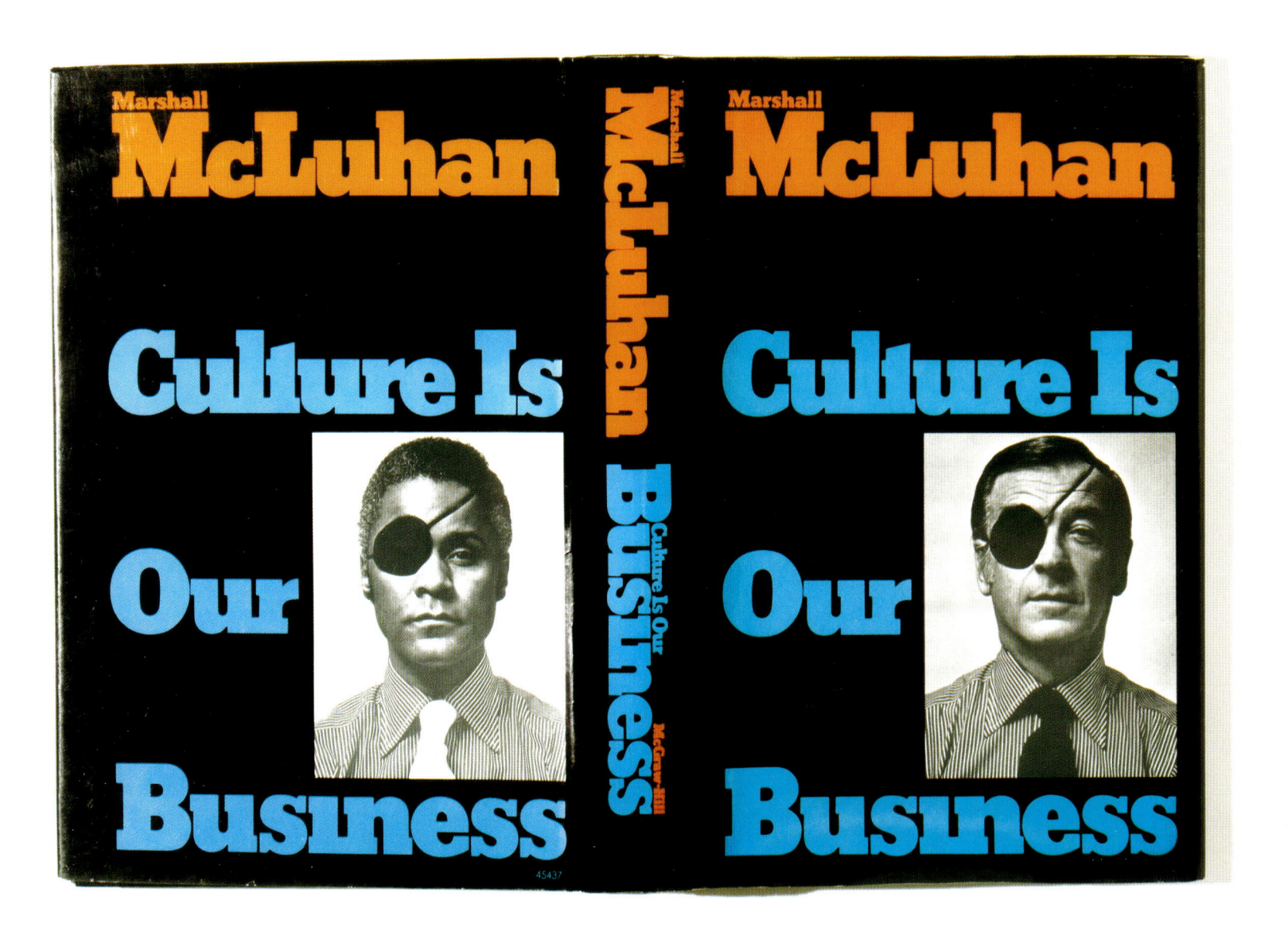

1990 Annual Report

New York City Partnership, Inc.
New York Chamber of Commerce and Industry, Inc.

The Partnership

Was founded in 1979 by David Rockefeller and other business leaders to tap the same kinds of energy and talent that New York's cultural, educational, and community service institutions have drawn upon for decades. Through its advocacy and its programs, it brings together leaders from business, city government, and community groups to help find solutions to problems affecting all of the New York City community.

The Chamber

Was founded in 1768 by local business leaders and is the oldest business organization in North America. Today the Chamber is the city's principal advocate for business. It lobbies in New York City, Albany and Washington on principles of concern to keep New York a desirable location for business, and operates, including The Chamber provides a range of programs, services and services for companies of all sizes to help them prosper and grow.

Chairman's Message
Preston Robert Tisch

The economic realities of 1990 and early 1991 were difficult for New York City, which suffered from corporate retrenchment and job losses. In addition, the slow state sector and local economy meant declining revenues for the city and state, both of which found themselves struggling to balance their budgets.

To many, these conditions were reminiscent of New York City in the mid-1970s fiscal crisis, when the city's financial problems led to tax increases, layoffs, and declines in services.

The New York City Partnership was founded in 1979 and allied with the New York Chamber of Commerce and Industry to broaden the cooperation among business, government and labor that was forged during that period. Working together, these groups helped restore that crisis. We are confident that with private and public sector collaboration, New York City will again solve its problems.

The Partnership and Chamber will continue to work to help the city and state balance their budgets...

President's Report
Ronald K. Shelp

Maintaining the city's economic base, thus insuring its ability to retain and create jobs for its residents, has always been a central priority for the Partnership and Chamber. Given current painful economic realities, this priority became even more critical in 1990 and will remain so...

The Partnership and the Chamber work to bring together the private sector and government to help make New York a better place in which to live, to work and to do business.

Helping Revive New York's Economy

Doom and Gloom

Inside: Building the Future Workforce... Creating Affordable Housing... and More...

EDUCATION

Building the Future Workforce

Recognizing that the success of New York's future workforce is critical to the city's economic growth, the Partnership's education efforts in 1990 focused on helping to prepare young people to meet the demands of today's information-intensive economy.

In addition to maintaining a series of successful programs, the Partnership was designated the New York City branch of Governor Cuomo's School and Business Alliance (SABA), a statewide consortium of business and educational leaders working to improve the employability of high school graduates. Partnership firms worked with the public school system as part of the Chancellor's innovative school-based management teams. They also conducted studies of the public school system's administrative functions to improve productivity and find savings. This year more than 30 Partnership firms participated in a year-long series of employability seminars initiated to help school personnel to better understand the demands of the workplace. Human resources professionals met with teachers, assistant principals and guidance counselors from schools throughout the five boroughs. These seminars helped school representatives understand the importance of teaching students the personal and social skills that are needed in a service and information-based economy, and helped corporate personnel officers to better understand the city school system and how students are being prepared for the job market.

The Partnership also conducted a survey of more than 100 corporations that led to the creation of "First Steps to Success," a guide to the qualifications they...

Creating Affordable...

By the end of 1990 the Partnership's New Homes Program—the city's largest private sector builder of affordable housing—had helped stimulate a total of $1 billion of private investment through both construction loans and permanent mortgages. It also helped create more than 6,000 units of affordable housing for moderate-income families in nearly 40 neighborhoods throughout the five boroughs.

Under the Partnership's housing program, the city provides low-cost land. The city, state and federal government provide subsidies to bring down the cost of each unit to make it affordable to middle-income families. The Partnership staff works with developers and banks to obtain the loans and financing, and supervises the administration of each project, including helping to obtain pre-development approvals and ensure subsidies for the homes. Local community groups serve as cosponsors of each project and help market the homes in their neighborhoods.

The Partnership's success in mobilizing private resources to support...

LEADERSHIP

Developing Tomorrow's Leaders

To help insure that New York maintains its place as a world financial and cultural capital, the city needs leaders in the private, non-profit and public sectors who understand and can help deal with difficult urban problems. Through its leadership development programs, the Partnership is working to ensure that the next generation of leaders in New York City is prepared to deal with these challenges.

The David Rockefeller Fellows Program was named after the Partnership's founding Chairman, who combined a distinguished private sector career with a lifelong commitment to social causes. The Fellows are all senior executives in their companies who devote significant portions of their time to public service, while they build their careers in business.

As an emerging focus of the program in its second year, the Fellows have been exploring the city's fiscal crisis of the 70's and how it compares with the current fiscal situation. The Fellows also met with the leadership of the Mayor's Management Advisory Task Force to discuss proposals to improve productivity in city government.

The Rockefeller Fellows have also participated in meetings and seminars led by the city's private and public sector leaders and experts in housing, health care, public safety, economic development and minority concerns. These meetings have included Mayor David Dinkins; Police Commissioner Lee Brown; Former Governor Hugh Carey; Willard C. Butcher, former CEO of Chase Manhattan Bank; Felix Rohatyn, partner at Lazard Freres and head of the Municipal Assistance Corporation; Stanley Hill, head of the municipal labor union District Council 37; Franklin Thomas, President, Ford Foundation; Peter C. Goldmark, Jr., President, Rockefeller Foundation; and Sol Wachtler, Chief Judge of the State of New York. In addition, the Fellows have met with representatives of the teachers union and local community leaders to learn more about the issues involving public school choice.

The Leadership New...

LEFT
For many years, I designed a traditional annual report, in both look and format, for this wonderful organization of extremely accomplished men and women who did consulting on various city projects. One year, I decided to change direction. I designed the report to look like a big city newspaper: It seemed like an obvious choice for a group that did timely projects for one of the biggest cities in the world. They reported that it was the most thoroughly read annual report that they had ever produced.

AT&T 1994 Annual Report

With 5% of the $1.5 trillion global information industry, AT&T is a small fish with lots of room to grow.

LEFT
For 1994's theme, AT&T wanted to tell shareholders that although it was big, it still had plenty of room for growth and innovation. I walked into our meeting and produced a white cover with some dummy type wrapped around a very small goldfish. The client jumped at the concept and wrote the copy on the spot that would eventually appear on the cover.

RIGHT
What a difference a year makes. Mid-creation of the 1995 annual report, AT&T was broken up into three separate companies. To provide a positive spin to shareholders, we had to totally re-conceive our strategy and cover. The solution speaks for itself.

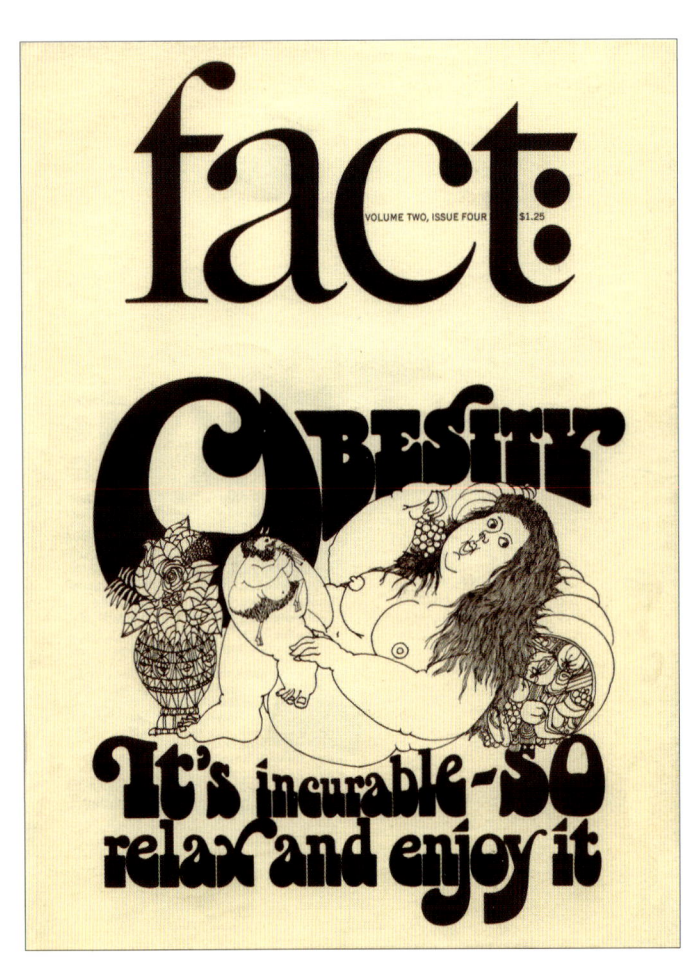

fact:

OBESITY
It's incurable—so relax and enjoy it

---

fact:

"The Star Spangled Banner is just so much trash." —Joan Baez

Westbrook Pegler: "I think The Star-Spangled Banner is just terrible." Louis Untermeyer: "The poets and composers of America could come up with something much better." Richard Rodgers: "It's impossible to sing." Marya Mannes: "Any musician will tell you it's a lousy piece of music." Meredith Willson: "It violates every single principle of song writing." Elmer Bernstein: "In today's world, we could do without warlike anthems like The Star-Spangled Banner." Godfrey Cambridge: "It has no meaning for the black man." LeRoi Jones: "It's pompous, hypocritical, vapid, and sterile." Fannie Hurst: "The Star-Spangled Banner, long may it _not_ wave!"

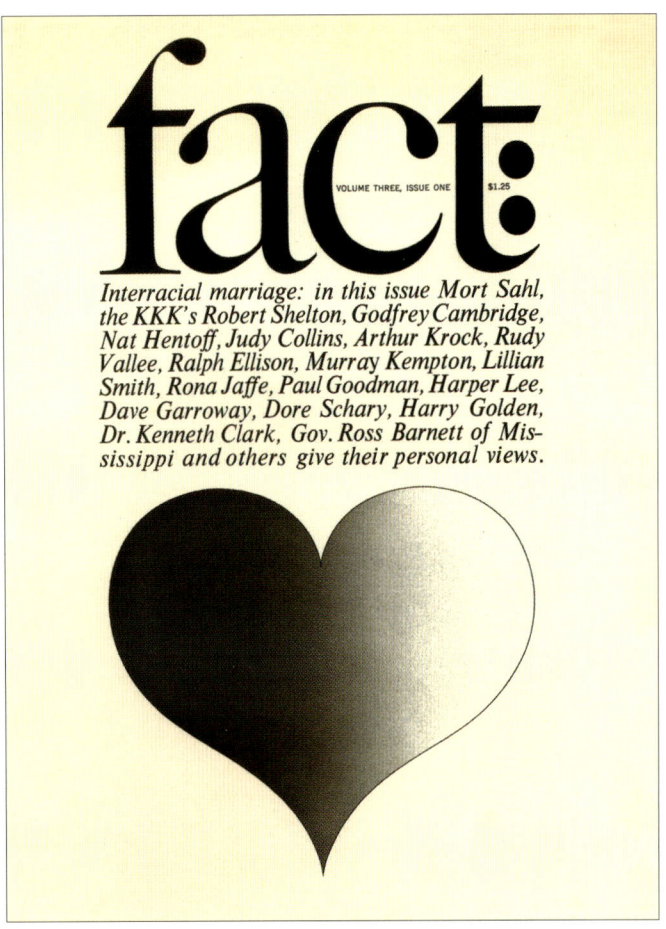

---

fact:

Interracial marriage: in this issue Mort Sahl, the KKK's Robert Shelton, Godfrey Cambridge, Nat Hentoff, Judy Collins, Arthur Krock, Rudy Vallee, Ralph Ellison, Murray Kempton, Lillian Smith, Rona Jaffe, Paul Goodman, Harper Lee, Dave Garroway, Dore Schary, Harry Golden, Dr. Kenneth Clark, Gov. Ross Barnett of Mississippi and others give their personal views.

ABOVE LEFT, ABOVE, AND LEFT
FACT, the seminal 1970s muckraking monthly magazine created by the brilliant Ralph Ginzburg, was one of our important clients. On my first morning at the studio, Herb Lubalin came in and gave me a cover to design. I was thrilled and a bit anxious. In the issue, *above*, famous people were asked if they felt the *Star-Spangled Banner* was an adequate national anthem. My tattered flag of type "talked."

BELOW RIGHT
Herb had a soft spot for designing liberal publications. *The New Leader*, originally conceived by faculty members from the New School for Social Research, contained intellectual editorials and essays by strictly left-wing writers. It had its debut in the 1920s and was one of Herb's favorite projects. Herb, who began designing the magazine in the early 1960s, handed it over to me a few years after I began working for him. I designed the magazine for over 20 years, and when the publication went to an online version a few years ago, the publisher came back to me and asked me to redesign it for the web—a lovely coda to a wonderful collaboration.

THE IRANIAN ELECTION WAS FAIR AND FREE

DUMB
IF YOU BELIEVE THE IRANIAN GOVERNMENT

PREVIOUS PAGES
In 2012, during the Iranian Revolution, an international group of graphic designers were contacted by dissidents who wanted to create a dialogue about the atrocities that were happening. My solution was simple and to the point, and "talked" about what Iranian freedom really meant to me.

RIGHT
The obvious image on this book cover is the star. As it was a history book, I made the type strong and direct. Case closed.

OPPOSITE
One of Herb's great pleasures was filling "O"s with images. Having been inspired by this, it was very easy to create this poster for the Hiroshima Peace Memorial Museum. My hope was that the final missing "O" would be very quiet.

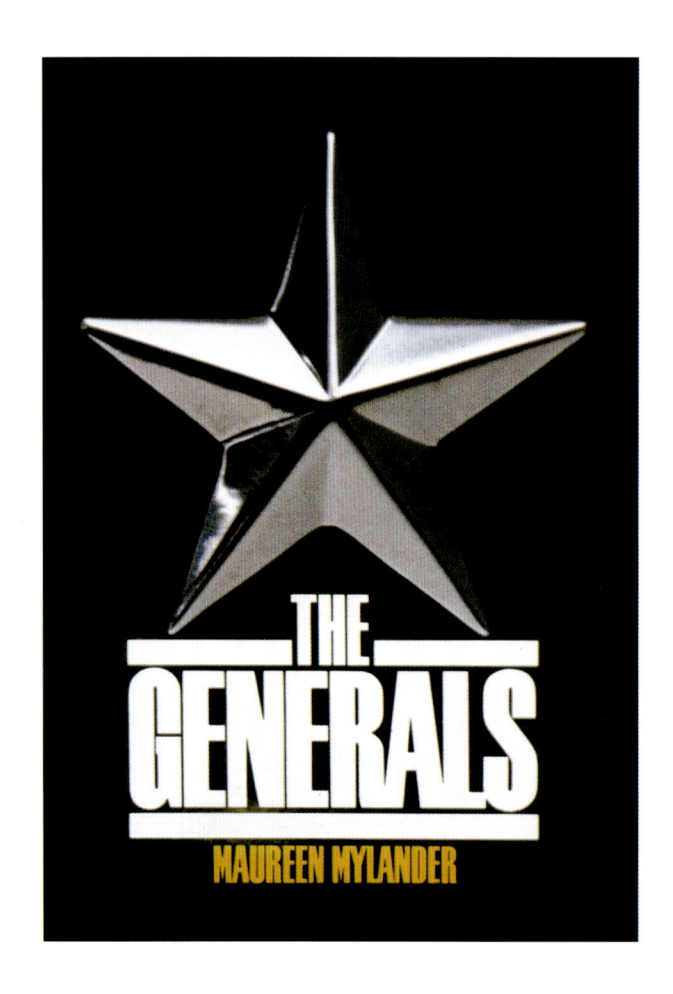

NO MORE WAR, OR JUST NO MORE!

Revised & Expanded

the A‑mer′i‑can Po‑lit′i‑cal Dic′tion‑a‑ry

**Jack C. Plano
Milton Greenberg**

LEFT
Sometimes the title of the book just leads you to the obvious solution. In this case, I wanted the cover to mimic the inside pages of a dictionary.

OPPOSITE
I asked a child to hand-letter the cover for me. The book was full of evocative drawings and paintings by children living in poverty in America. I made sure the type was minimal, not invasive, and let the artwork do the talking.

THE WORLD FROM MY WINDOW

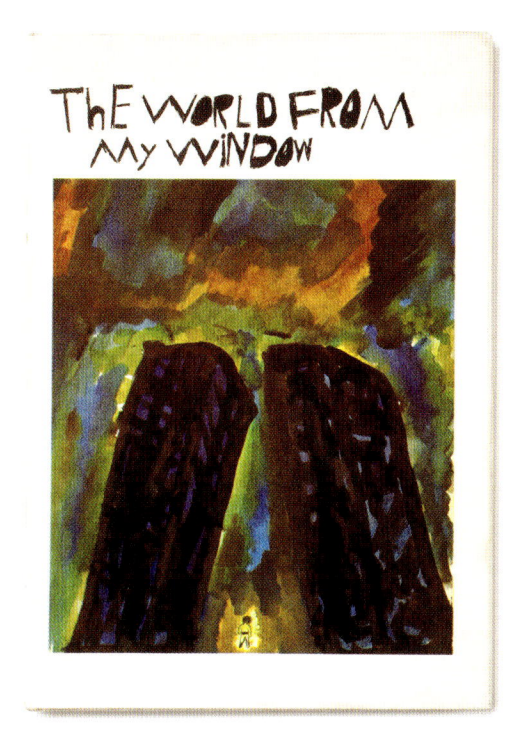

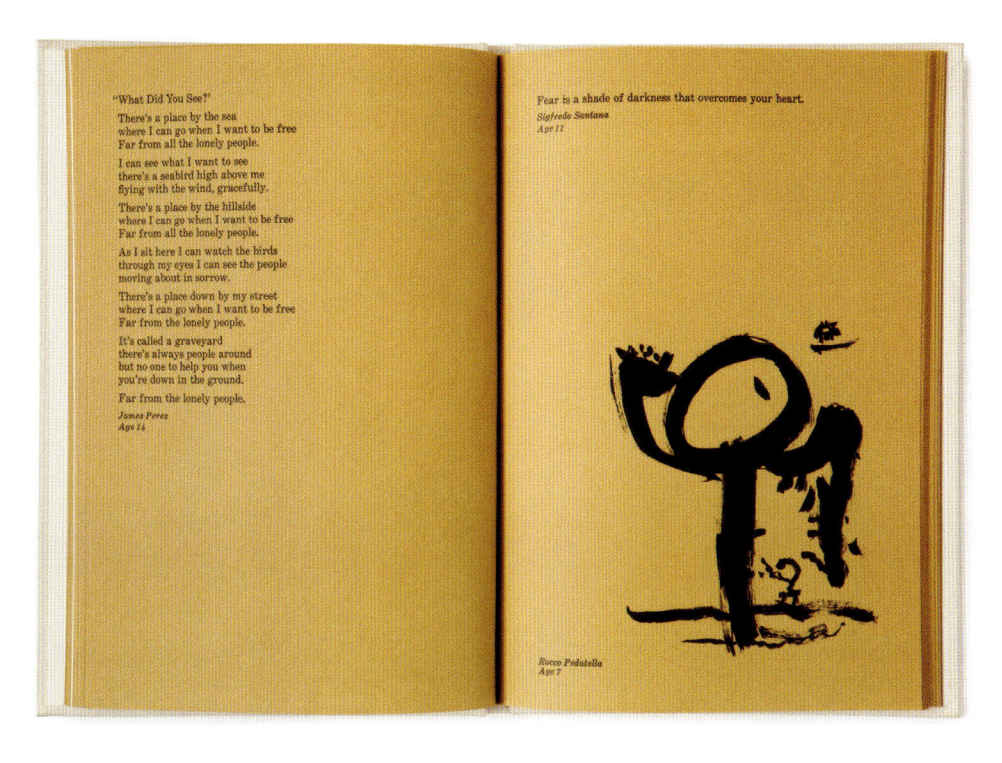

In 1974, a publisher friend of mine brought me to Washington, D.C., to meet a potential new client. When we arrived, I was going to look for a taxi, but he said a car was picking us up. A few moments later, I saw a rather long black limousine with White House markings on the doors coming in our direction. My friend turned to me and said: "The First Lady has a project for you. I'm here to make the introduction." We met Pat Nixon, the wife of President Richard Nixon, at the White House. She told me she had seen several books that I had designed, in particular *The World from My Window*, and wanted me to create a souvenir book highlighting the achievements of the President's first term. It was to be distributed for free at the Republican National Convention, as part of Nixon's campaign for a second term. As she spoke, all I could think about was that there was no way this book could help elect a president, not to mention that I didn't want to help re-elect this particular one. So when I got a call from Mrs. Nixon's assistant a few days later, telling me she now wanted the book to be longer than originally planned and sold to raise money for his campaign, I said thanks, but no thanks. Before this, the most radical thing I had done was to wear loafers with my tuxedo.

3. HOLLY-WOOD CALLING

Hollywood rhymes with magic, at least in my mind. I must admit that I am starstruck and always have been. From the lights of Broadway to the sounds of a backroom club, our thirst for entertainment never seems to subside. In the 1960s and 1970s, the Hollywood dream factories would engage

D several design studios to work on the same big budget film, picking and choosing elements from one studio and mixing them up with those from others. I personally didn't like working in a professional shootout. But I still had to pay the rent.

SIMON WIESENTHAL CENTER
AT YESHIVA UNIVERSITY
OF LOS ANGELES PRESENTS

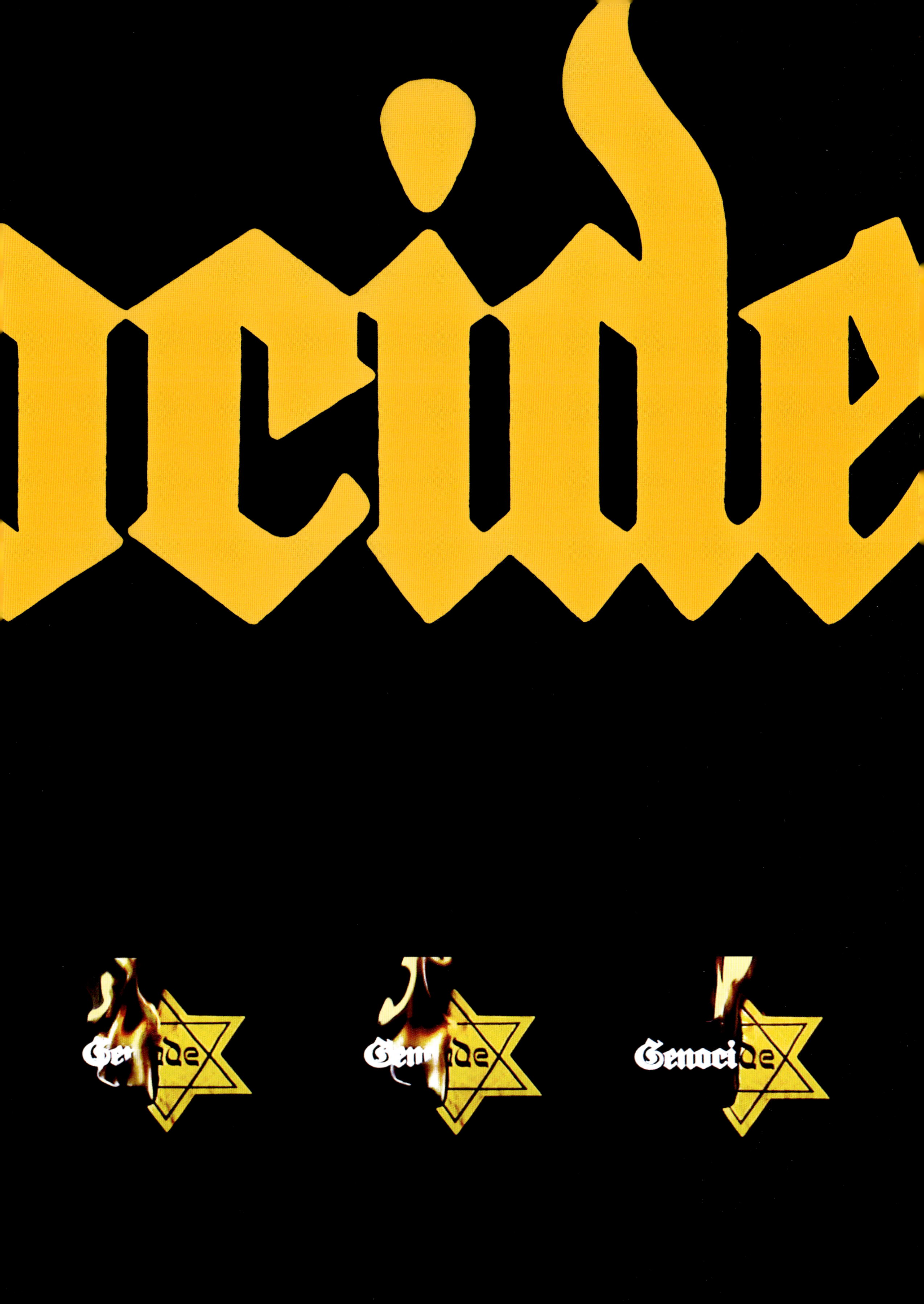
ocide
Genocide

PREVIOUS PAGES
I got a call from my friend Arnold Schwartzman, a brilliant graphic designer and filmmaker in Los Angeles. He asked me to create a logo for a film that he was making for the Simon Wiesenthal Foundation, called *Genocide*. I agreed immediately. My goal was to create the word "genocide" to look as if it had been designed during the time of the Holocaust. I researched German publications from that era. In the opening sequence, the Star of David becomes engulfed in flames, burning away to reveal the title of the film behind it. The film went on to win the 1982 Academy Award for Best Documentary Full-Length Feature. I am very proud to have been a part of it.

OPPOSITE AND LEFT
When I met graphic designer and filmmaker Saul Bass for the first time, it felt as if we had known each other forever. I was enamored by his film title sequences and his stories of old Hollywood. He liked the way I designed and used type. Plus, we both grew up in the Bronx. From that day on, we were pals. He always called me Butch, and from time to time I was sure he forgot my real name. Many times over the years, Saul tried to lure me out to the West Coast to head his design office. One day in the early 1980s, I got a call from him: "Hey Butch, want to work on a project with me?" He had just designed a logo for the Kaufman Astoria Studios, a new film studio in Queens, New York. The client needed signage and someone to oversee their print graphics, and since Los Angeles, where Saul was stationed, was too far away, he introduced me as his head designer in New York. The next day, I became the studio's design consultant. They needed a brochure that had two purposes—to promote both stage and staff rentals, as well as a multitude of other print materials. Because the studio was hidden away in an old factory complex, it was also impossible to find the entrance to the place. I designed the banner to make the location more noticeable, silk-screening Saul's logo and an image of a piece of film going through a sprocket onto them.

the BAND the LAST WALTZ

OPPOSITE
Director Martin Scorsese asked me to create a logo for *The Last Waltz*, his documentary film on The Band's last concert performance, which was released in 1976, and asked me to go to California for a rough-cut screening at the MGM Studios in Los Angeles. I was beyond thrilled to have the opportunity to work with Scorsese, not to mention being utterly starstruck. At the screening, to which Scorsese invited only his closest friends, I found myself sitting directly behind Jack Nicholson. I missed great chunks of the film because I spent the time staring at the back of his head. After the film ended, I told Scorsese it was fantastic and that I would love to work on the project, but that I would need to bring a copy back to New York with me to watch it a few more times in detail.

BELOW
My involvement with Jack Nicholson didn't end there: I ended up designing the poster and logo for his 1978 Western romantic comedy and directorial debut, *Goin' South*. The "T" in "South" extends like a lasso to form the shape of a heart. The problem with working with film people is that by the time they give you a project, they are already two projects ahead of you and aren't focused on that one anymore. The only way I could communicate with Nicholson's people directly was by telephone, after midnight, E.S.T., when I could have their full attention.

"Jesus help me, cause man won't."

Short eyes

Miguel Pinero's SHORT EYES
Starring Bruce Davison and Jose Perez
Also Starring Nathan George, Don Blakely,
Shawn Elliott, Miguel Pinero, Joseph Carberry,
Tito Goya and Kenneth Steward
Guest Stars Curtis Mayfield and Freddie Fender

Directed by Robert M. Young
Screenplay by Miguel Pinero
Music Scored and Composed by Curtis Mayfield
Photography by Peter Sova

Produced by Lewis Harris
Executive Producer Marvin Stuart
Edited by Ed Beyer
A Film League Presentation

R RESTRICTED

OPPOSITE
I was approached by the Film League, a group of young Hollywood producers, to do a poster for the 1977 film *Short Eyes*, a dark and true story about an imprisoned pedophile. As a low-budget, low-distribution independent production, they wanted something dynamic to match the high-budget look of the big studios, like Warner Brothers or MGM.

RIGHT
I designed the logo, record jacket, and posters for musician Paul Simon's album and movie, *One Trick Pony*, which came out in 1980. I used the typeface Avant Garde Latin with pointy serifs, which had never been released to the public, and broke up the word "One-Trick" with a hyphen. It's strong, in your face, and the right look.

OVERLEAF
For the poster for the 1964 World War II film *Weekend at Dunkirk*, Tom Carnese (my partner and brilliant hand letterer) and I designed the original letter-forms and then cut them up with a razor blade to get the effect, literally shattering the letters to evoke the horror and violence of war. This European production was never released in the United States.

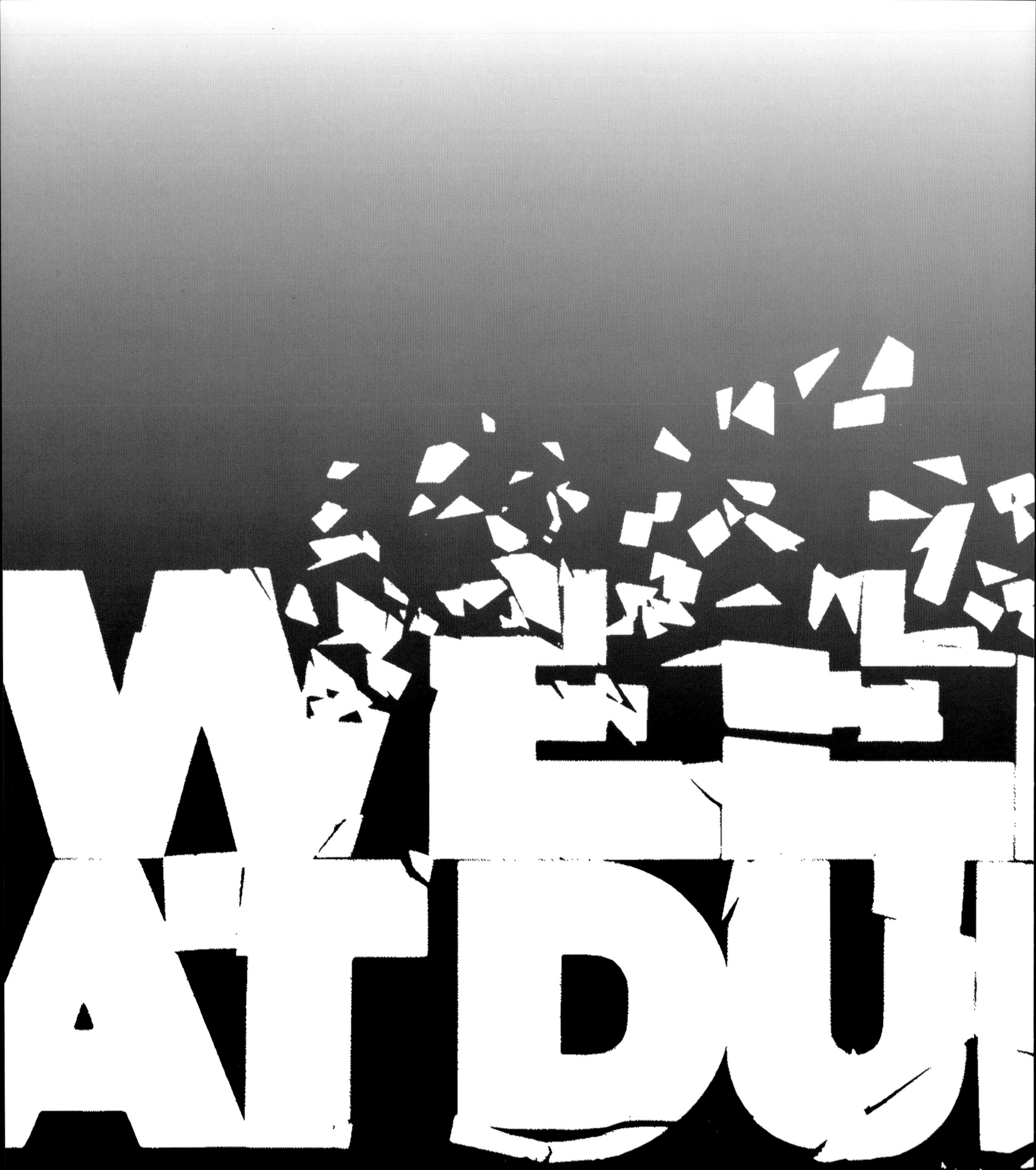
WE
AT DU

KENDWRK

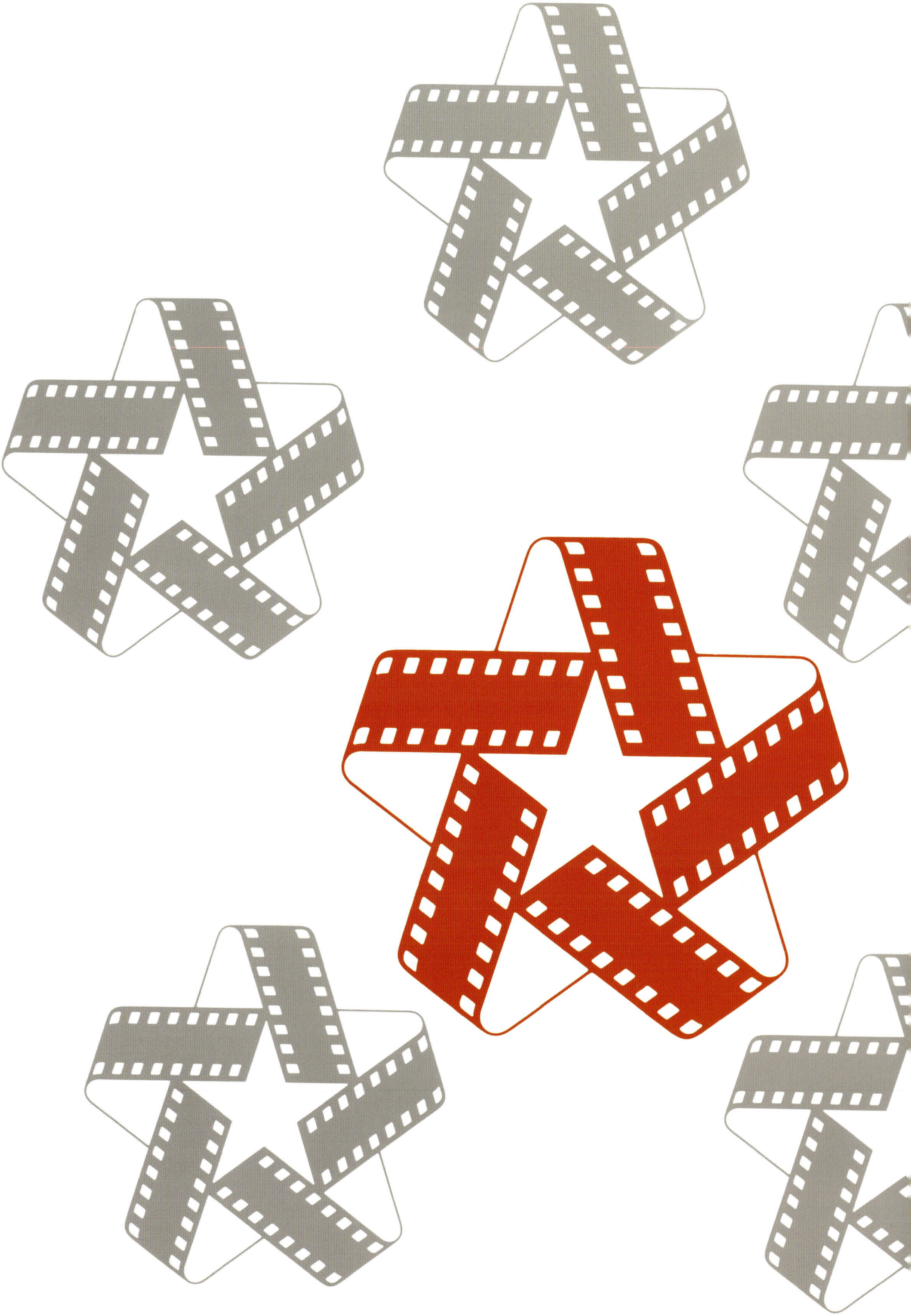

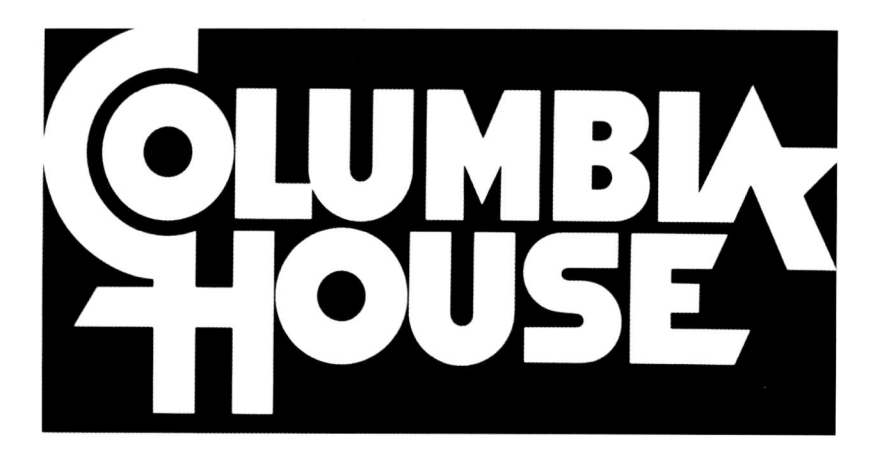

ABOVE
The star shape in the logo for the mail-order music club Columbia House, and its Canadian division, introduced in the 1970s by Columbia Records, subtly indicates their involvement in the entertainment business.

LEFT
When the Time Warner company asked me to create a logo for a new cable station that it was launching to play first-run movies, and which would be named Star Channel, I designed a star made out of film strips. Though the company ended up changing the station's name to The Film Channel, it still used my logo. It didn't seem to matter that the logo no longer really suited the name.

ATLANTIC GALLERY

ABOVE
The Atlantic Gallery is a cooperative gallery of contemporary artists in New York to which I belong. Like its aesthetic, the lettering is clean, fresh, and modern.

OPPOSITE
For the brochure for a Polish short-film festival, organized by McGraw-Hill, I used a different typeface to express the variety of genres that was represented.

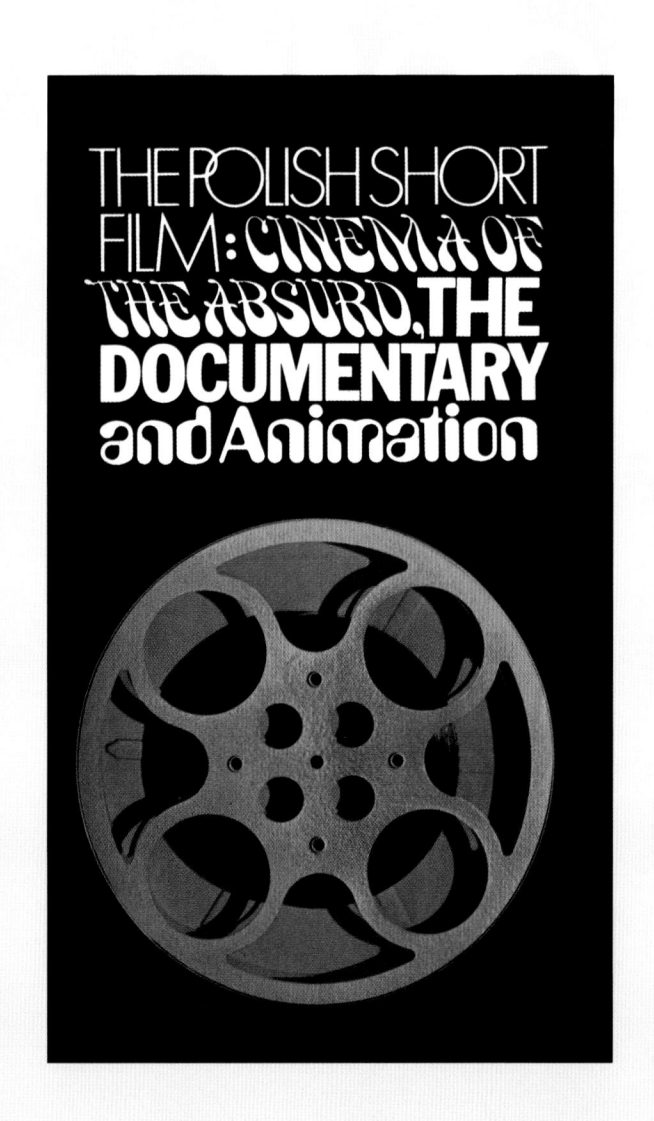

THE POLISH SHORT FILM: CINEMA OF THE ABSURD, THE DOCUMENTARY and Animation

LEFT
The Mobil Corporation asked me to produce a poster for a series of programs on PBS that it was sponsoring about love, called *All For Love*. The design and romantic typeface in red is mine, but the idea to use an assortment of dictionary definitions of love actually came from the client's wife.

OPPOSITE
Another poster for Mobil announced their funding of three museums in New York—The Museum of American Folk Art, The Whitney Museum of American Art, and the Guggenheim Museum—to allow them to stay open late and to be free to the public on Tuesday evenings. My idea was to create a graphic design that would suggest a work of contemporary art, keeping the colors minimal and using three different shades of blue.

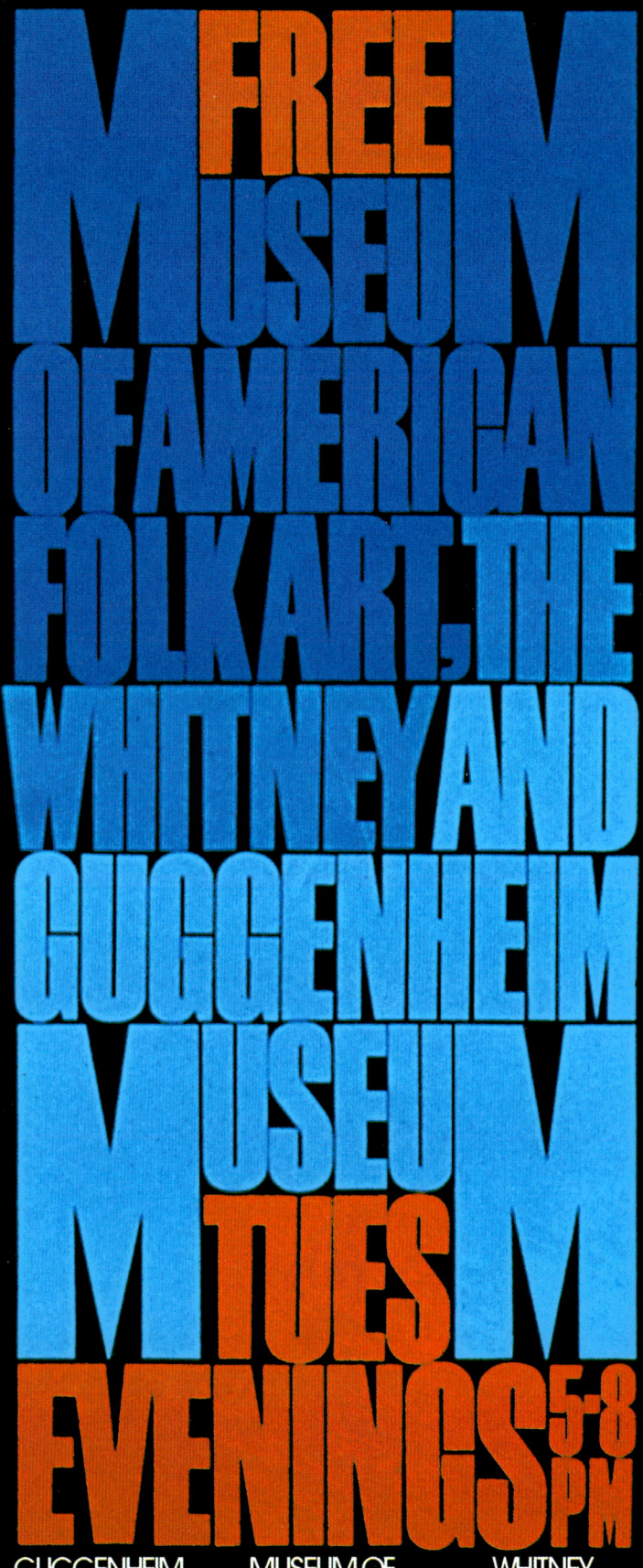

FREE MUSEUM OF AMERICAN FOLK ART, THE WHITNEY AND GUGGENHEIM MUSEUM TUES EVENINGS 5-8 PM

GUGGENHEIM MUSEUM
89 ST. & FIFTH AVE.

MUSEUM OF AMERICAN FOLK ART
49 WEST 53 ST.

WHITNEY MUSEUM
75 ST. & MADISON

MADE POSSIBLE BY A GRANT FROM
Mobil

AMERICAN STAGE

JUNE 1977 — PRICE $2.00

"THIS CHAMPIONSHIP SEASON" OUTFRONT WITH CLIVE BARNES
NEW WAVE OF PLAYWRIGHTS BY RICHARD BARR
COMPLETE PLAYSCRIPT: "GEMINI"
"LITTLE ORPHAN MIKE" BY MEL GUSSOW

Annie's Mike Nichols

THESE PAGES
Herb Lubalin and I were asked to design a prototype for what was the first serious theater magazine at the time, which was to be called *American Stage*. It was to feature every level of theater. Lubalin created the logo, and I designed the layouts. For the cover, I slapped director Mike Nichols' head on Little Orphan Annie's body to attract readers.

RIGHT
A gatefold spread features the actors in a performance of *A Chorus Line*, with their biographies listed beneath them.

106

107

Stomping the Blues

ALBERT MURRAY

DUKE • BESSIE • LOUIS • BIRD • LESTER • JELLY

THESE PAGES AND OVERLEAF *Stomping the Blues* is a history of the blues by Albert Murray published in 1976. I wanted the cover to resemble the label that used to be affixed to old 78-rpm long-play vinyl records. The theme and logo were carried through to the interior pages, *overleaf*, as wheels on a train.

109

Musicraft
REG. U.S. PAT. OFF.
MARCA REGISTRADA
461
HAPPY GO LUCKY LOCAL
from "The Deep South Suite"
(Ellington)
DUKE ELLINGTON
and his
FAMOUS ORCHESTRA
BLUEBIRD
Electrically
PHONOGRAPH
Recorded
RECORDS
Not Licensed for
Radio Broadcast
HOBO YOU CAN'T RIDE THIS TRAIN Fox Trot
(L. Armstrong)
Louis Armstrong and his Orchestra
Vocal refrain and trumpet solo
by Louis Armstrong
B 6501 B
©RCA Manufacturing Co., Inc. Camden N.J. U.S.A.

27235-B
BLUES-Fox Trot
VICTOR
"HIS MASTER'S VOICE"
24501-A
DAYBREAK EXPRESS—Fox Trot
(Expreso Madrugador)
(D. Ellington)
Duke Ellington and his Orchestra
Aladdin
HOLLYWOOD CALIFORNIA
WOR 1684
Vocal · 3:00
DETOUR AHEAD
(Frigo - Carter - Ellis)
BILLIE HOLIDAY
(Lady Day)
with
TINY GRIMES' SEXTET
3094

4. DEAL WITH SUITS

You can call them bean counters, clients, or just plain suits, but they are corporate executives who hold the purse-strings and the power to accept or reject a designer's best creative efforts. I never forget that they know more about their business than I ever will. Something I picked up early on: Never talk to a suit about design. In most cases, he or she will think you're talking basket weaving. My clients come to me not for design, but because I'm a professional problem-solver who just happens to use design as a tool. I translate their business problems into design solutions. Our work together is all about communicating and meeting our respective right-brain and left-brain perspectives in the middle.

HIGH POTENCY
CALCIUM
SUPPLEMENT
500 MG
OS-CAL
500
100
TABLETS

THESE PAGES
The client asked us to create an interesting and memorable package for Os-Cal, their top-selling calcium supplement, that would separate their product from the others in that category. I came up with an idea that abstractly suggested a human bone. The client accepted the idea on the spot, but after being cautioned by their advertising agency to test the design before making any commitments, they held some focus groups in the Midwest. The only thing we learned was that some Midwestern housewives have extraordinarily erotic imaginations. They went with plan B.

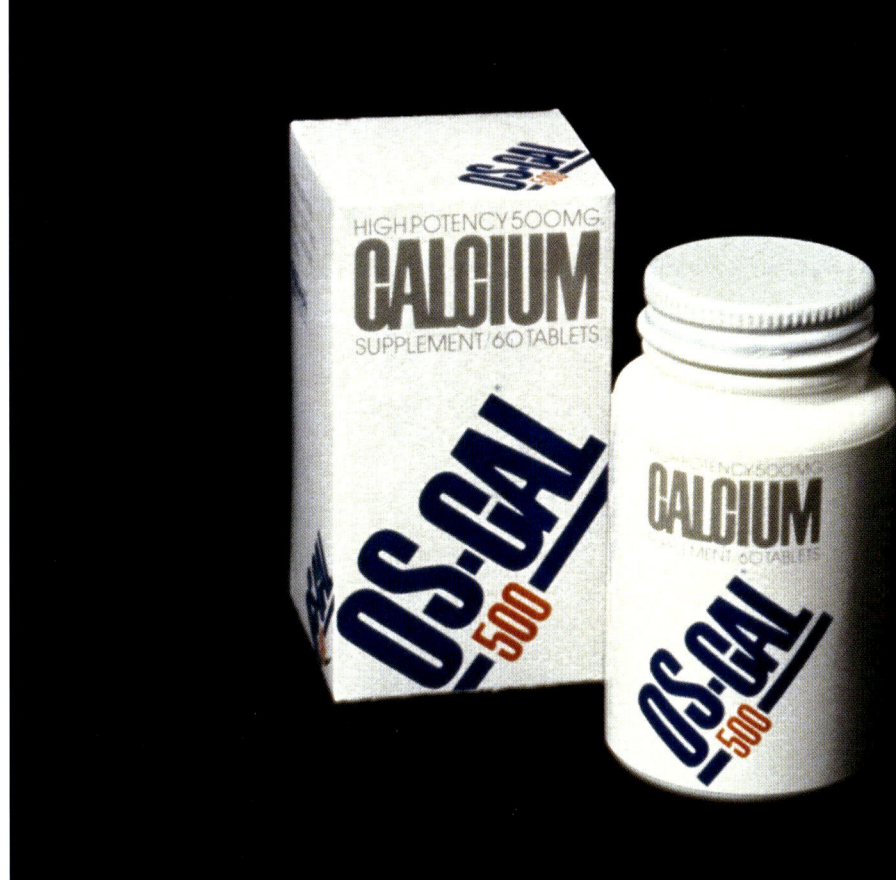

THESE PAGES AND OVERLEAF
Ebasco, the Electric Bond and Share Company, which provided engineering, consulting, and construction services, asked me to design a promotional booklet that presented its projects. They wanted it to represent them with a contemporary, corporate look that was engaging and easy to read.

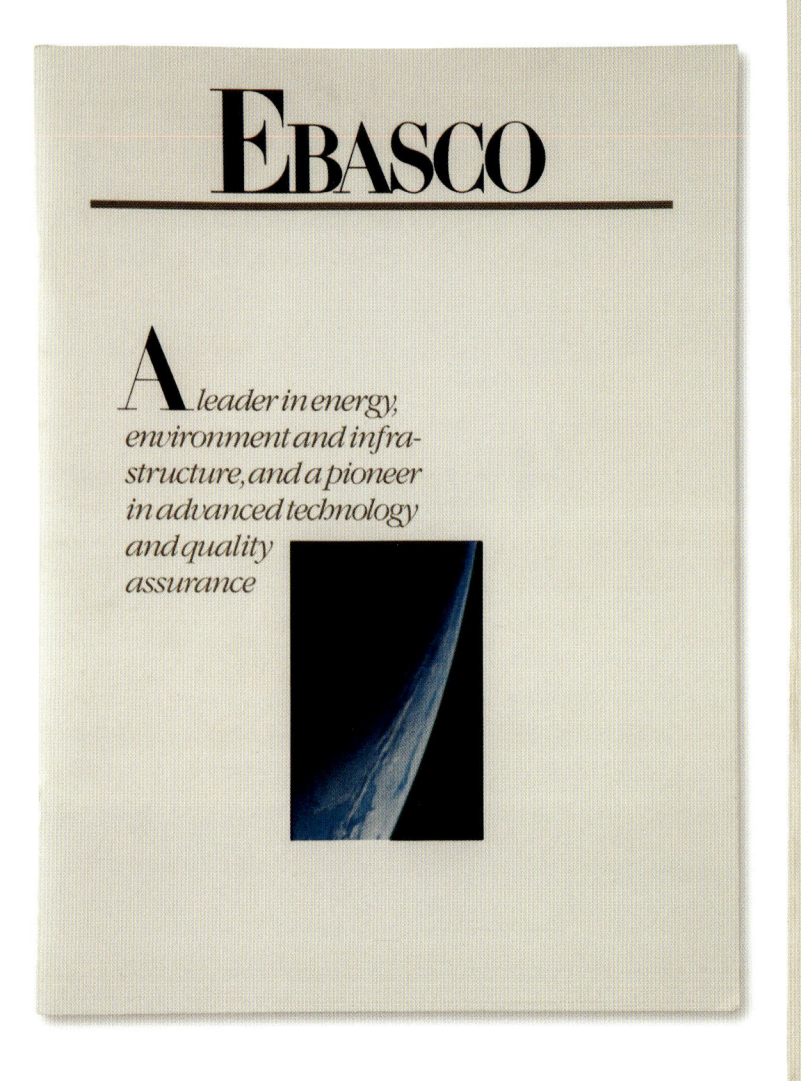

EBASCO

A leader in energy, environment and infrastructure, and a pioneer in advanced technology and quality assurance

"Ebasco Services has extended far beyond their contractual agreement; you get what you pay for and then some. It is this extra effort by Ebasco that has been the key to our success. Ebasco has effectively monitored construction progress…Their commitment to quality in overseeing the Harris County Toll Road project played a major role in timely completion and substantial budget reductions."

Wesley E. Freise
Executive Director
Harris County, Texas
Toll Road Authority

...RASTRUCTURE

Whether it's a tunnel, transportation system, building or dam, Ebasco brings to each infrastructure project unique, full-service capabilities. Our comprehensive experience in civil, military, industrial and power project engineering and construction is world renowned.

For two consecutive years, *Engineering News-Record* (ENR), the leading industry publication, has ranked us "number one" in heavy civil construction.

In 1989, Ebasco set two speed-drilling records for a 15-foot diameter hard-rock tunnel in Alaska. We also began more than six miles of 12- and 32-foot diameter flood-control tunnels, 200 feet under Chicago's heavily populated western suburbs.

Ebasco has been involved in the development and rehabilitation of all types of military facilities. We provided construction management services for the homeporting of the U.S. Navy Northeast Battleship Surface Action Group at Staten Island. The project is one of the most extensive undertaken by the Navy.

During the past 80 years, we have completed thousands of projects in more than 60 countries, including a wide range of infrastructure projects. In India, Sri Lanka, Peru, Colombia and Brazil, we retrofitted U.S. embassies to help protect them against terrorist attack. And in Georgetown, Guyana, we are constructing a new embassy, one of the first to be built under the provisions of the Omnibus Diplomatic Security and Antiterrorism Act.

Ebasco maintains offices abroad and in major U.S. metropolitan areas. This enables us to respond efficiently to the needs of federal, state, municipal and foreign governments, and to tailor projects to fit local requirements.

For example, Ebasco's ability to manage the massive construction of the Harris County, Texas, Toll Road, one of the largest roadway projects ever undertaken in the United States, demonstrates the array of skills the company brings to infrastructure projects. Ebasco developed engineering contracts, schedules and cost contr... $900 million project, mo... work in progress, and ne... agreements among variou... government agencies. Br... worldwide project mana... experience and understa... the design and constructi... process have enabled us t... complete the toll road on... track schedule.

Homeport Staten Island is one of the Navy's most extensive infrastructure p...

Marshall Space Flight Center

Excelling in quality assurance

Ebasco was selected in 1988 to provide on-going quality management services for the Marshall Space Flight Center in Huntsville, Alabama. The assignment embraces the shuttle program, the space station, Spacelab, the tethered satellite system and the Hubble Space Telescope.

For four decades, Ebasco has pioneered quality assurance standards. Its successful techniques were originally developed in the power industry. Ebasco's Corporate Quality Programs division responds to clients in the public and private sectors, including the aerospace, electronics and computer industries, as well as 15 other markets.

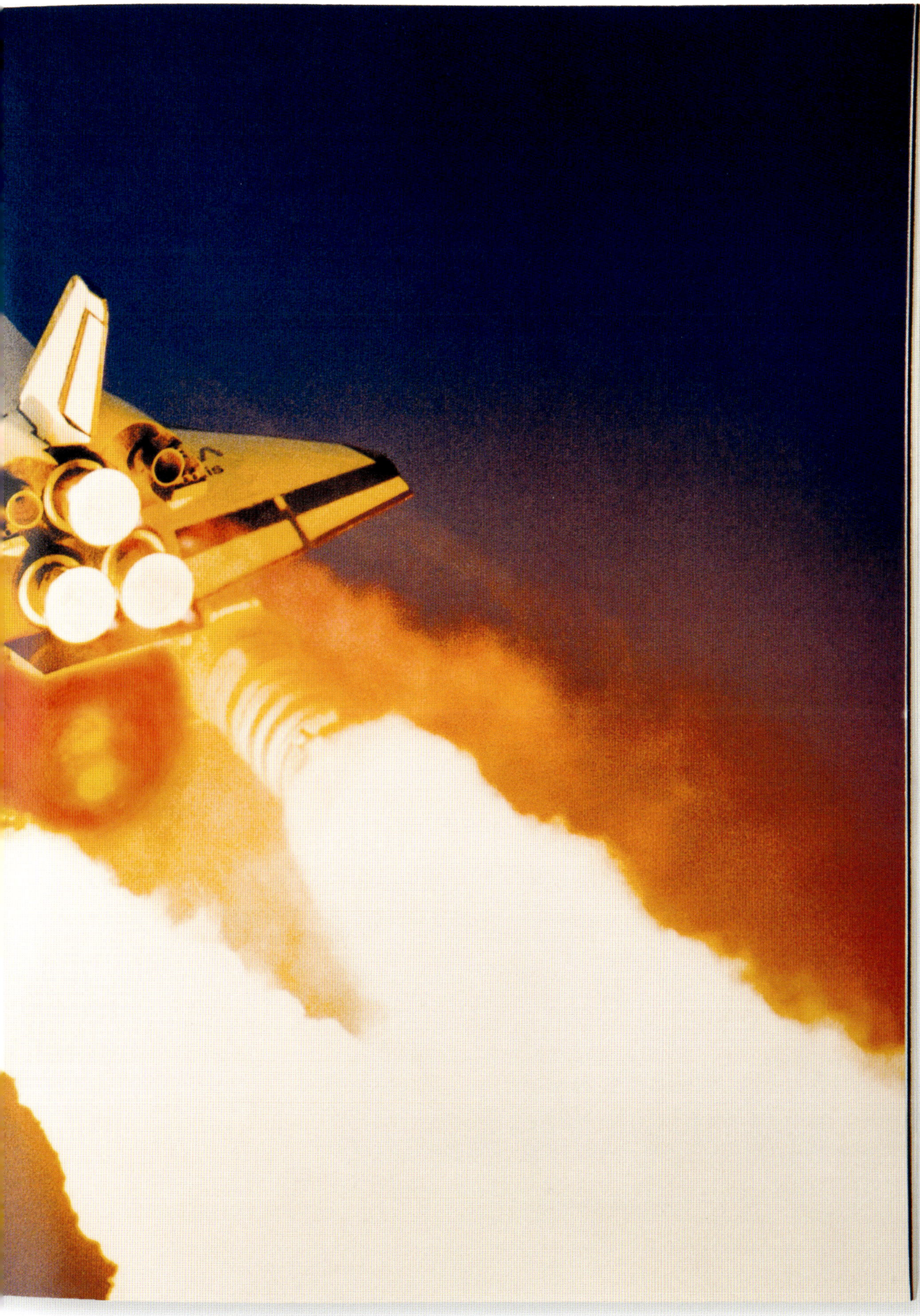

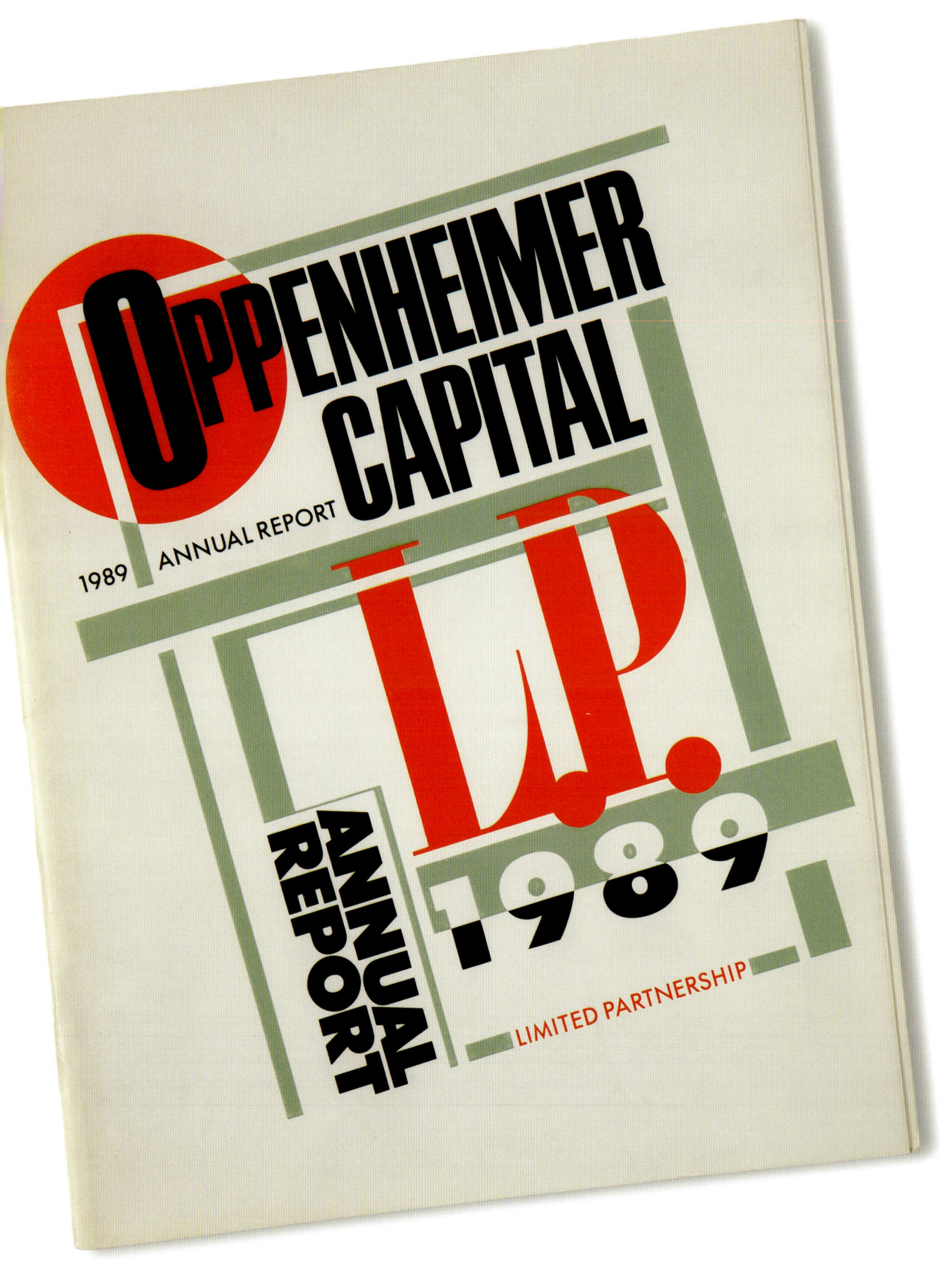

Oppenheimer Capital

1989 ANNUAL REPORT

L.P.

Annual Report 1989

LIMITED PARTNERSHIP

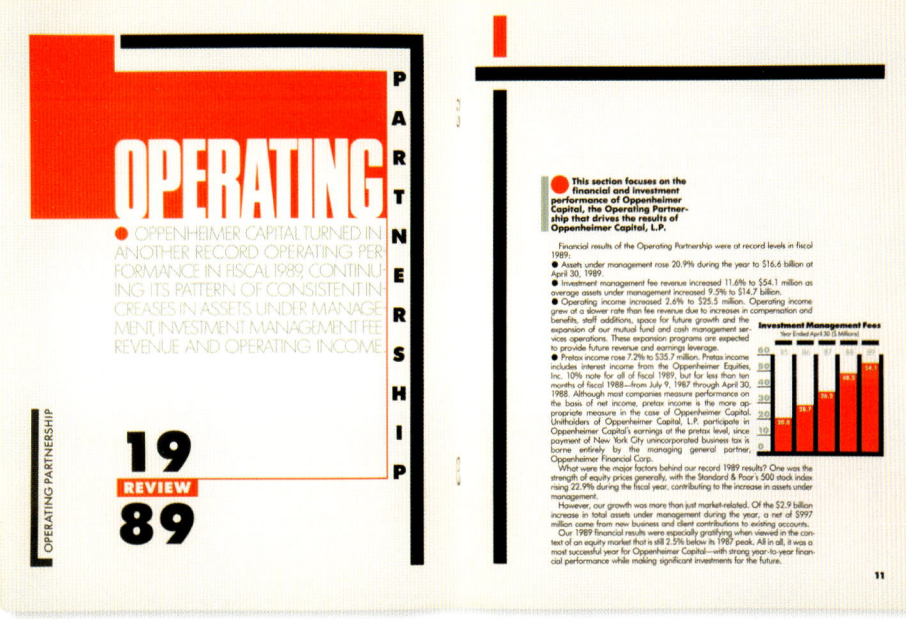

THESE PAGES
AND OVERLEAF
In 1988, I was asked to design the annual report for Oppenheimer Capital, a leading capital markets firm. At my first meeting with Joseph M. La Motta, the CEO, he told me his problem was simple. Because of the nature of business and government regulations, he said he couldn't say anything differently in the reports than his competitors. But he really wanted to be different. He told me he had heard that I was a typographic virtuoso. "Prove it!" he said, "Do a good job on this year's report, and you will get next year's." The project was like a breath of fresh air to me because I didn't design it with a specific concept. Instead, I focused solely on its design and aesthetics, using typography in a decorative manner to make the cover of the report distinctive. In this way, clients would be able to differentiate Oppenheimer Capital's annual reports from others. My goal was to give their annual reports a specific, recognizable, and memorable personality. And it worked. Both La Motta and his clients loved it, and I ended up producing ten annual reports for him after that. Lesson learned: Never put financials in red.

I separated the leading capital markets firm Oppenheimer Capital from its competition by giving the annual reports a unique, contemporary, and bold design. The black 1988 cover was the first to land us many years of work.

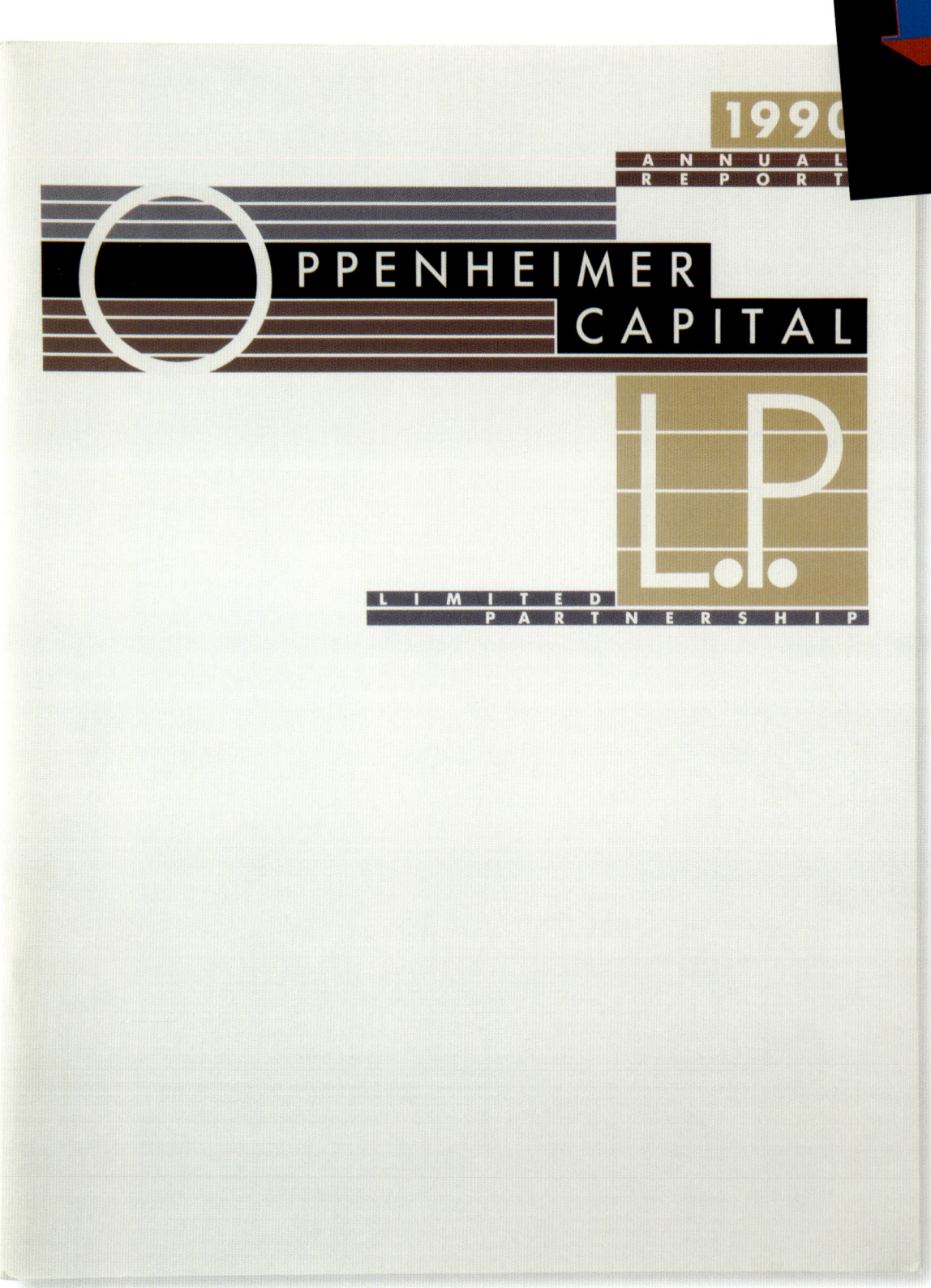

OPPENHEIMER CAPITAL, L.P.

1·9·9·2 ANNUAL REPORT

LIMITED PARTNERSHIP

THESE AND FOLLOWING PAGES Grupo Industrial Alfa, the largest business conglomerate in Mexico, does everything from manufacturing motorcycles, to owning hotels and spas, to processing meat and cheese. GIA wanted their annual report to look like the company was as contemporary and up-to-date as big American companies. They also wanted to shed the image of being a stereotypical Mexican company. I designed a book entitled *Modern Mexico* to accompany the annual report that presented Mexico as a sophisticated and thriving nation. This was accomplished with beautiful double-page spreads illustrating Mexican systems, such as healthcare, government, and infrastructure. The annual report was packaged in a presentation box with an intricate ethnic Mexican pattern that I designed after a wooden box that the client gave me as a gift.

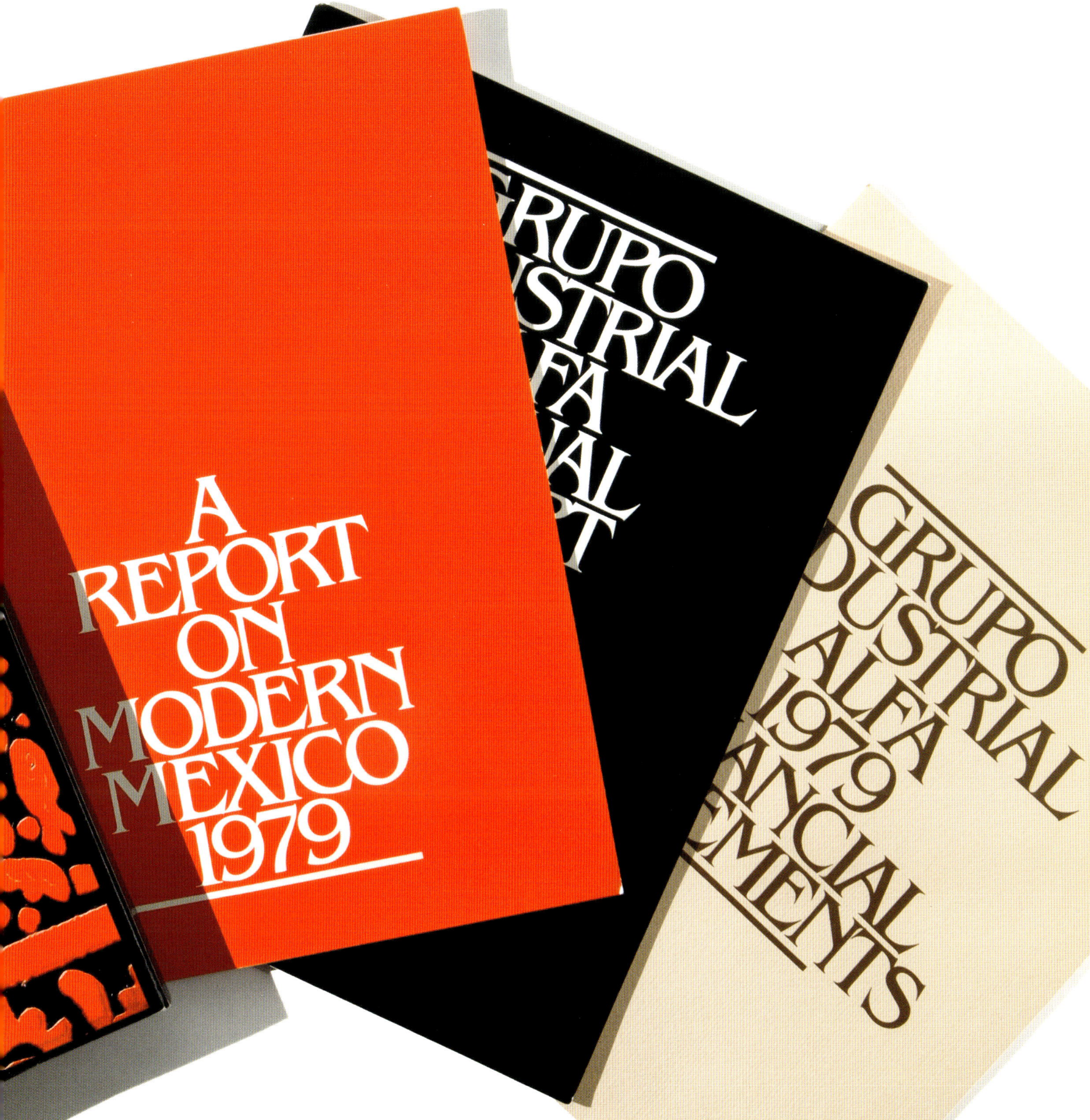
A
REPORT
ON
MODERN
MEXICO
1979
GRUPO
GRUPO
ALFA
1979

ALFA AT A GLANCE

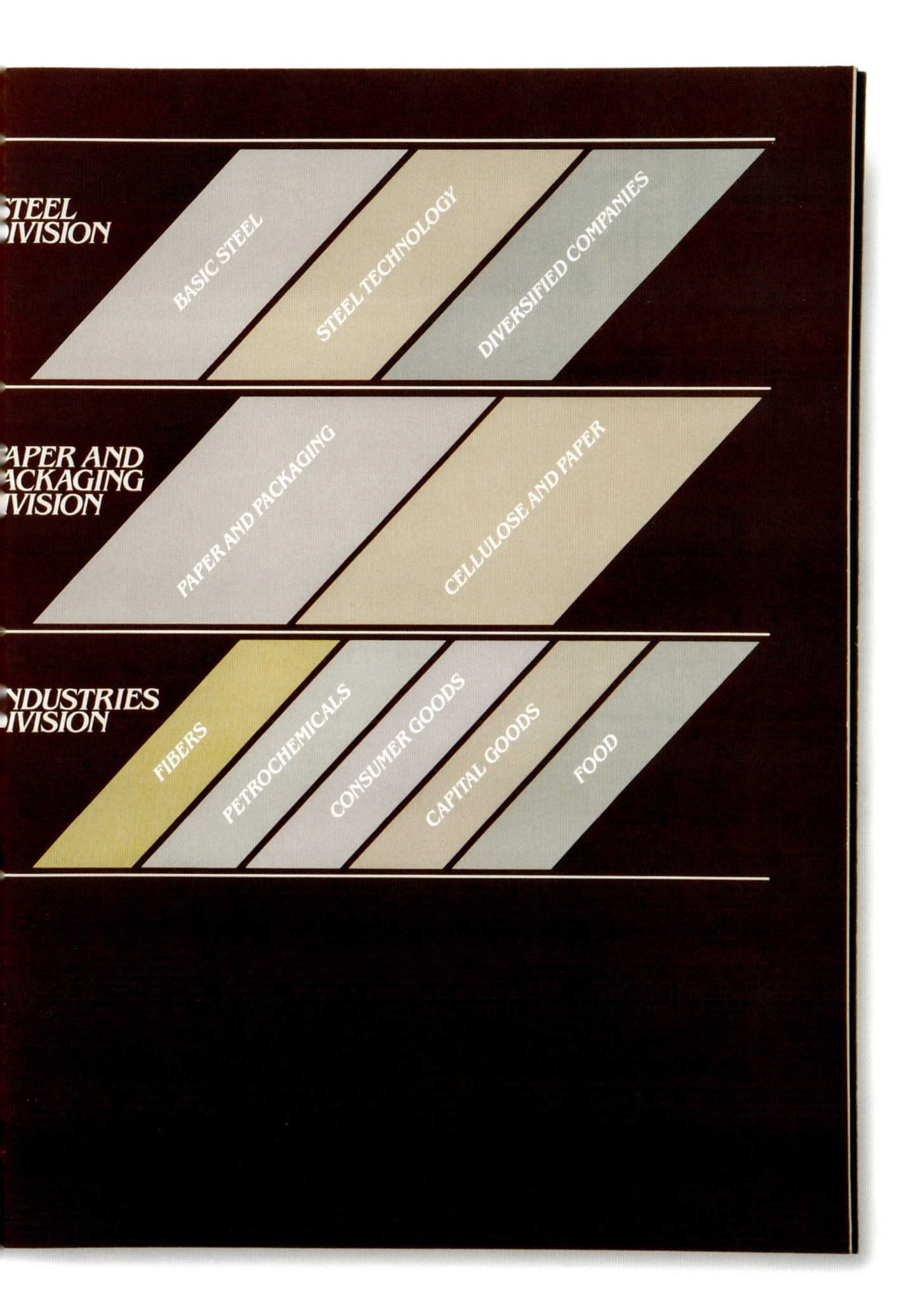

STEEL DIVISION
- BASIC STEEL
- STEEL TECHNOLOGY
- DIVERSIFIED COMPANIES

PAPER AND PACKAGING DIVISION
- PAPER AND PACKAGING
- CELLULOSE AND PAPER

INDUSTRIES DIVISION
- FIBERS
- PETROCHEMICALS
- CONSUMER GOODS
- CAPITAL GOODS
- FOOD

EXPANSION OF ALFA

COMPANY	DATE	PRODUCTS
Steel Division		Flat Steels
Hylsa	Pre-1974	Structural Steels
		Steel Technology (Worldwide)
HYL	Pre-1974	Diversified Companies
Hymax	1975	Galvanized Sheet Metal
—Galvak	1978	Specialty Steels
—Atlax (on stream 1981)	1979	Industrial Equipment and Machinery
—Makros, (on stream 1980)	1979	
Paper & Packaging Division		Paper and Packaging
Titán	Pre-1974	Cellulose and Paper
Celulósicos Centauro	1979	
Industries Division		Non-ferrous Metals
Draco	1975	Land and Resort Development
Casolar	1975	Polyester Yarn
Akra (Nylmex & Fiqusa)	1975 & 1977	Polyester Staple
		Nylon Yarn
		Industrial Nylon
		Spandex
		Rugs and Carpets
Carpet Project (on stream 1980)	1979	Ethylene Glycols
Polioles	1975	Industrial Polyols
		Expandable Polyestyrene
		Urethane Polyols
Petrocel	1978	DMT (Dimethyl Terephthalate) & TPA (Terephthalic Acid)
POM	1979	Polyurethane and Thermoplastic Shoe Soles
		Mattresses
Selther	1979	Polyurethane Foam
		Color Televisions
Philco*	1976	Black & White Televisions
Admiral*	1978	Stereo Consoles
Magnavox* *(The products represent Philco, Admiral and Magnavox combined)	1979	Hi-Fi Modular Equipment
		Auto Radios
		Motorcycles
Acer-Mex	1979	Bicycles
		Agricultural Tractors
Agromak (Massey Ferguson)	1979	Industrial—Agricultural Diesels
	1979	Combines
		Agricultural Implements
		Electric Home Appliances
Vistar (on stream 1981)	1979	Processed Meats
Food	1980	Fresh Meats
(beginning January 1980)		Communications
Televisa (25% ownership)		
Administrative offices**	Pre-1974	

**Includes: Alfa Steel Division, Alfa Paper and Packaging Division, Alfa Industries Division, Alfa Dinamica and other services.

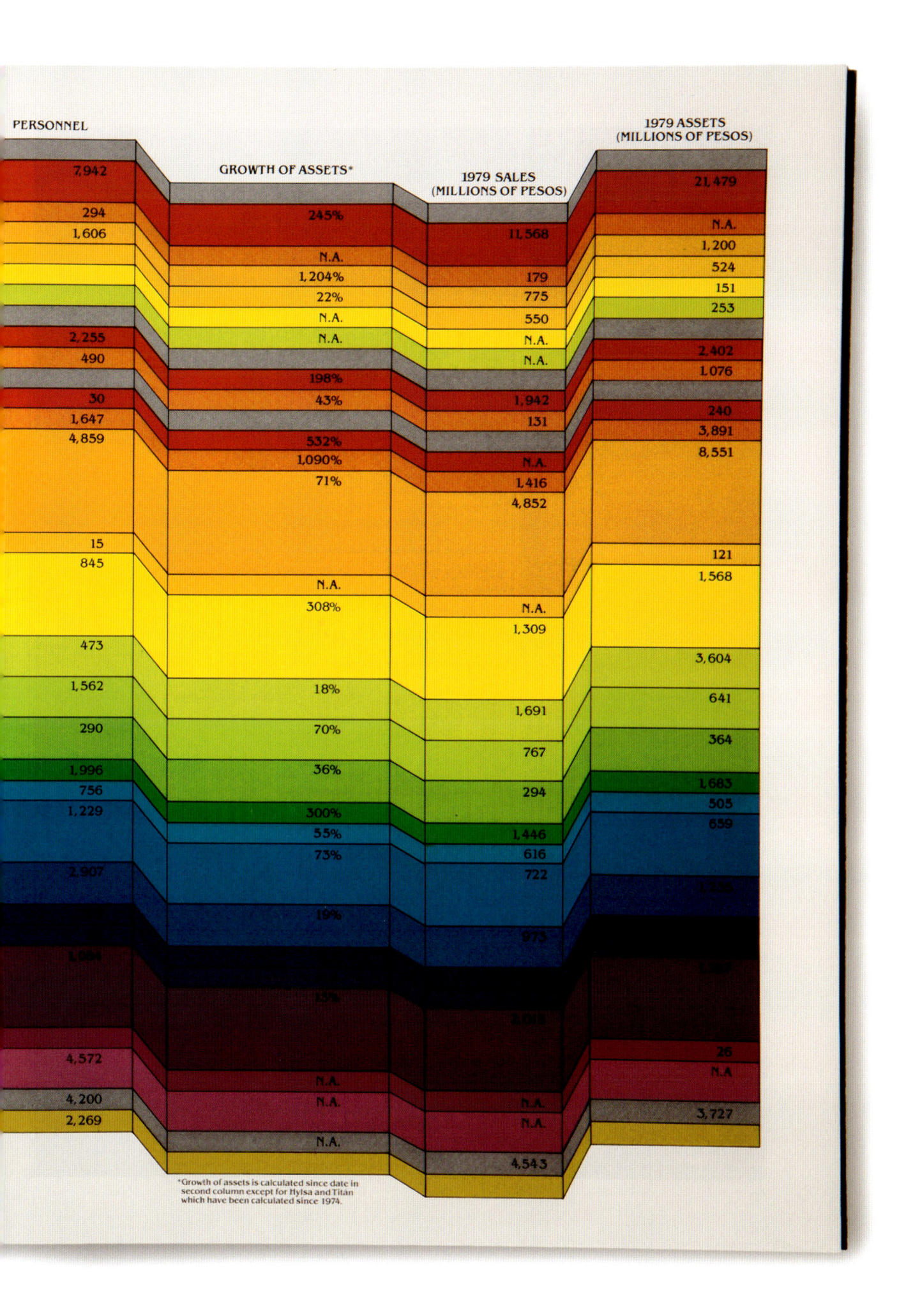

PERSONNEL	GROWTH OF ASSETS*	1979 SALES (MILLIONS OF PESOS)	1979 ASSETS (MILLIONS OF PESOS)
7,942			21,479
294	245%	11,568	N.A.
1,606	N.A.		1,200
	1,204%	179	524
	22%	775	151
	N.A.	550	253
2,255	N.A.	N.A.	2,402
490	N.A.	N.A.	1,076
	198%		
30	43%	1,942	240
1,647		131	3,891
4,859	532%		8,551
	1,090%	N.A.	
	71%	1,416	
		4,852	
15			121
845			1,568
	N.A.	N.A.	
	308%	1,309	
473			3,604
1,562	18%		641
		1,691	
290	70%	767	364
1,996	36%		1,683
756		294	505
1,229	300%		659
	55%	1,446	
	73%	616	
2,907		722	1,236
	19%	975	
1,084	15%	2,018	
4,572			26
	N.A.		N.A.
4,200	N.A.	N.A.	3,727
2,269		N.A.	
	N.A.	4,543	

*Growth of assets is calculated since date in second column except for Hylsa and Titan which have been calculated since 1974.

INFRASTRUCTURE

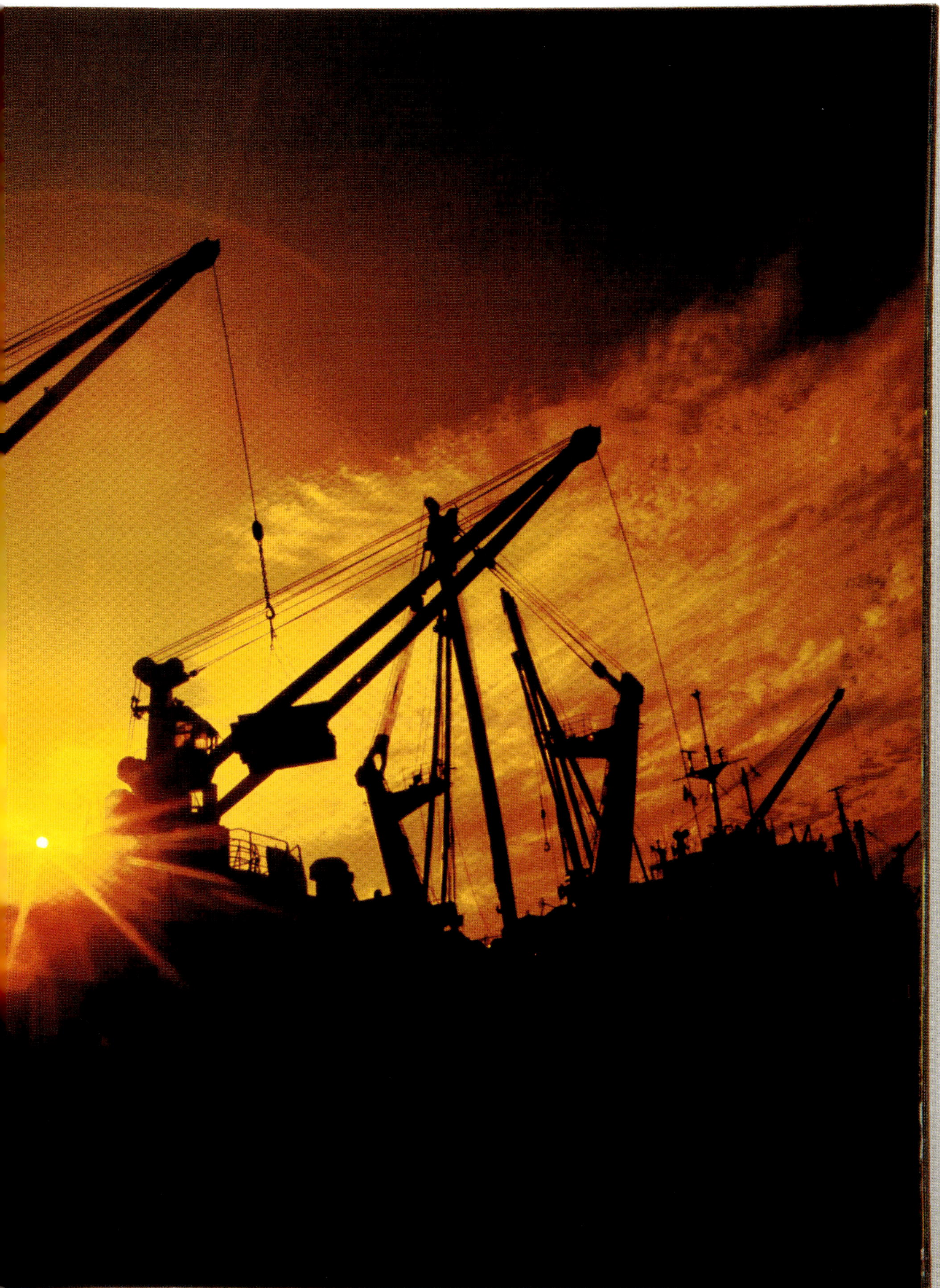

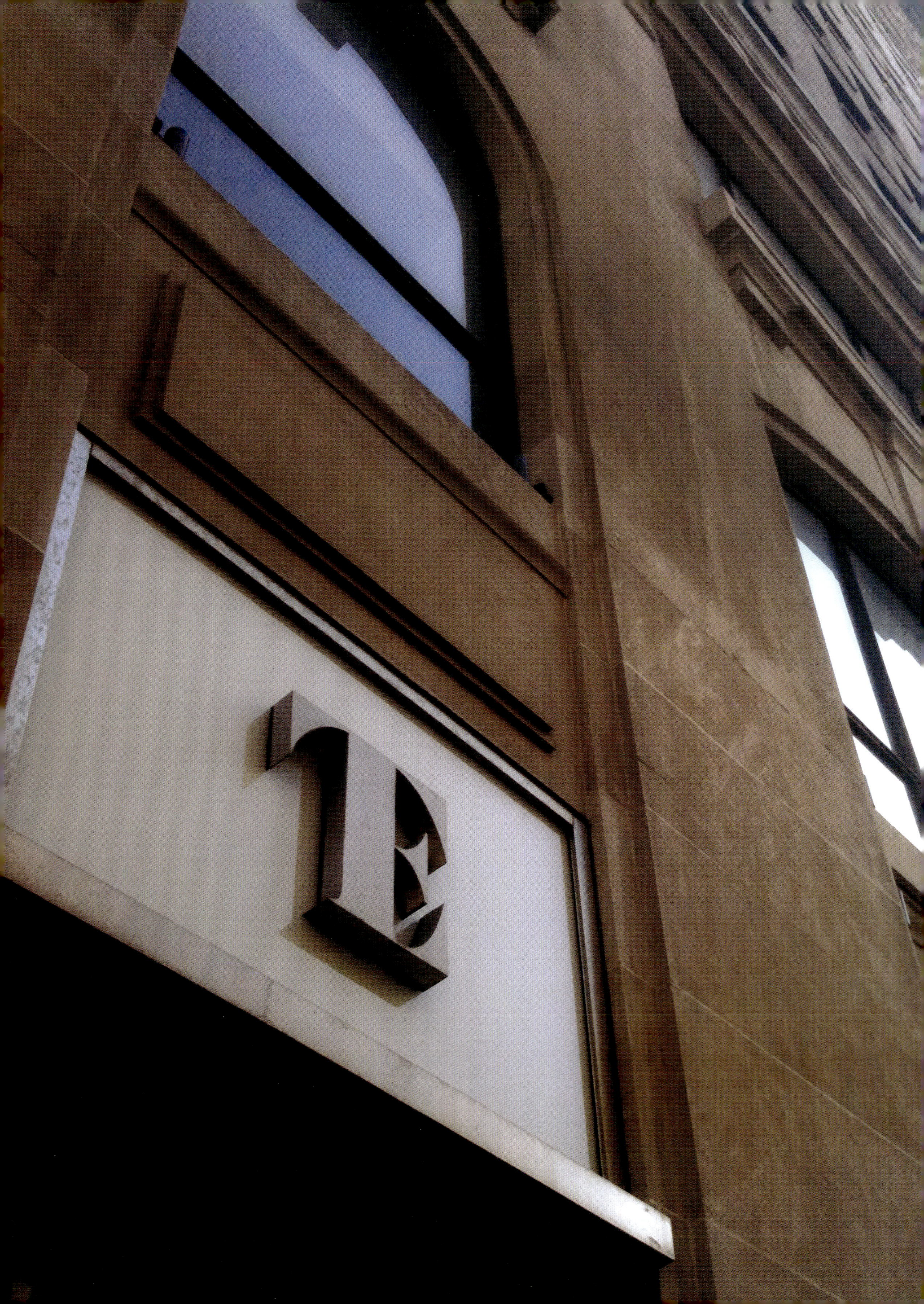

OPPOSITE
One of the earliest projects I ever did was for the New York-based real estate company, Time Equities, Inc., when my first office space was in the same building. I liked their space better than the one I was going to take so we made a deal to switch. I melded their initials by overlapping the letters' serifs.

ABOVE
The American Savings Bank didn't want their logo to resemble what people typically expect a bank logo to look like. I merged the "A" in American with the shape of a star to create this unconventional graphic identity.

18
+

BELOW
The client wanted an English language identity for a worldwide banking association called 18 Bank. I linked the two words with the 8, which I split to also function as the B.

Bank
八銀行

LEFT
After seeing my logo for 18 Bank, another Japanese bank called to have me create a non-typographic symbol that represented the four elements in Japanese philosophy, and the bank's core beliefs—earth, water, fire, and wind.

BELOW
The letterforms of the S.G. initials of this European bank chain fit together naturally. When merging letterforms, they must look comfortable and natural together. I either make the fit very tight or allow for certain spaces.

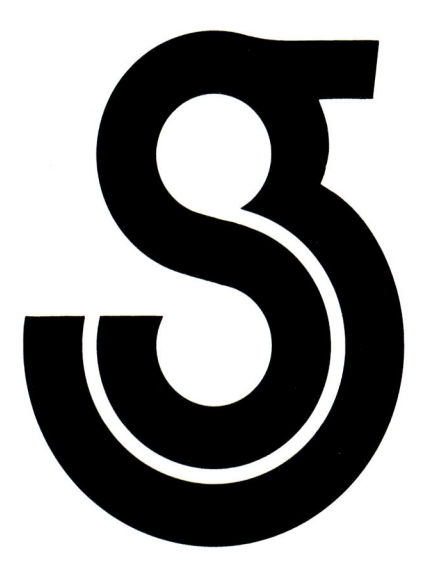

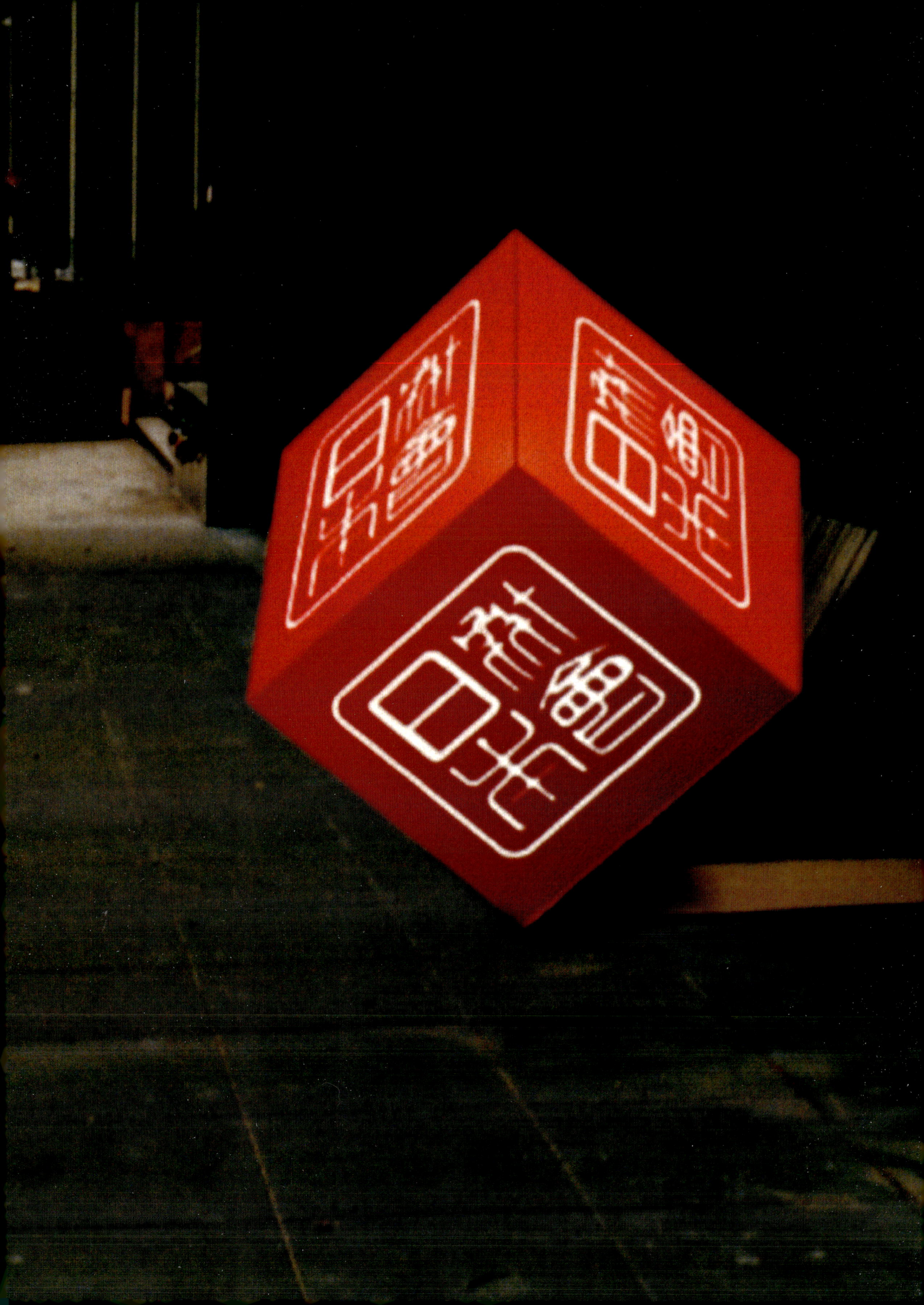

OPPOSITE
The Japan Society had no visual presence on a conventional midtown block near the United Nations Building in Manhattan. Using Japanese letterforms (their chop), I designed this cube as a bold and sculptural brand identifier.

BELOW
I'm always bothered when I see an "r" and a "u" next to each other with too much space between them. When I was asked to redesign the Baruch College logo, I got the chance to solve the problem.

Baruch
COLLEGE

©1998 Baruch College/The City University of New York.

Baruch

ROM@N

! @ # $ % & * ( ) ? ;

B

Aa Bb Cc Dd
Ee Ff Gg Hh
Kk Ll Mm Nn
Oo Pp Qq Rr
Ss Tt Uu Vv
Ww Xx Yy Zz

City

GOT#IC

C

! @ # $ % & * ( ) ? ;

Aa Bb Cc Dd
Ee Ff Gg Hh
Kk Ll Mm Nn
Oo Pp Qq Rr
Ss Tt Uu Vv
Ww Xx Yy Zz

the City College of New York

PREVIOUS PAGES
I designed the two proprietary typefaces for Baruch College, in New York, *left*, and the City College of New York, *right*, and which I called Baruch Roman and City Roman, respectively. They were used on all the printed materials and provided the backbone for the schools' corporate personalities.

OPPOSITE
The president of the City College of New York wanted to distinguish the school from the other city universities. In his brief he wanted the word "the" emphasized. I accomplished this by enlarging it, raising it above the other words, and giving it a different background color.

RIGHT
The logo for Nassau Community College, in Garden City, New York, is distinctive and scholarly.

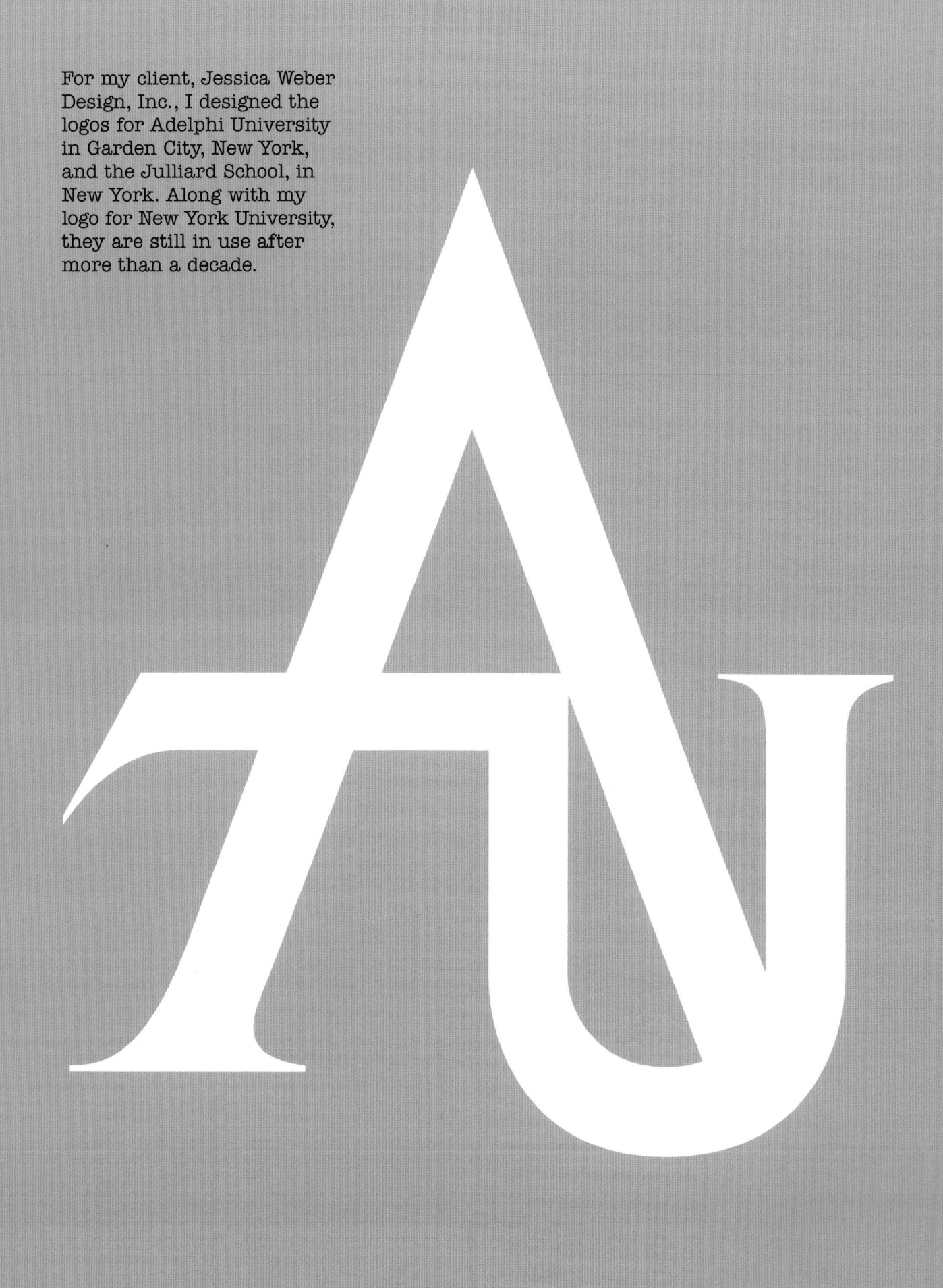

For my client, Jessica Weber Design, Inc., I designed the logos for Adelphi University in Garden City, New York, and the Julliard School, in New York. Along with my logo for New York University, they are still in use after more than a decade.

NEW YORK UNIVERSITY

OPPOSITE
For Adelphi, part of the problem was to figure out what not to do. The name itself conjures up such tired graphics—Greek columns, torches, flags, etc. I went the other way, with crisp, clean, and modern letterforms, which I joined in a unique fashion to become classic in itself.

ABOVE
Because New York University has so many different schools, I had to create an umbrella identity that would cover all of them, from film to business to medicine. In fact, Allan Beaver, the creative director of the advertising agency Levine Huntley Schmidt & Beaver, is no slouch himself when it comes to words and graphics. As soon as he gave me this project, he seemed to visualize what my solution would be. I used the basic typeface Times Roman and modified the characters, creating ligatures between the "U" and "N," and the "R" and "S." And because everyone refers to the school as NYU, I made those three letters stand out from the rest of the characters by making them slightly larger. It's sophisticated, elegant, and distinguished.

BELOW
After my first presentation of ideas, I knew we had an extremely conservative client. I followed suit. I used a classic typeface called Clearface, which allowed me to create ligatures—the only option I had to keep this logo from being just another line of set type.

Juilliard

5. IN YOUR FACE

In today's highly competitive environment, we are constantly being bombarded with visual messages. Time and time again, products ask us to buy them, drive them, watch them, read them, and eat them. In a world of endless options and variety, how does anyone choose one product over another?

It's my job to help the consumer make the right decision. Once again, I call on typography—as the designer—to give the product a unique look. While the packaging may say something about the product, it also says something about the purchaser. We are what we buy. It is up to the company to manufacture the product, and it's up to the designer to manufacture the image.

REV

LON

asics

PREVIOUS PAGES
I designed the corporate trademark for the mega cosmetics company Revlon Inc. However, since Revlon is also an umbrella organization for non-cosmetic products, I didn't want to make the logo too feminine—it had to be able to more broadly represent all aspects of the company. I connected the "L" and the "O" for smooth pronunciation.

LEFT
Herb Lubalin and I designed the logo for ASICS, the manufacturer and seller of sports goods.

OPPOSITE
A company that produces menswear came to the Lubalin Peckolick studio, wanting us to create a brand for their new line of socks. After doing test marketing, it found that men typically don't think of socks as articles of clothing, or even as attached to any particular brand. Herb and I conceived of the name "Toes Clothes" and packaged each pair of socks separately in a plastic sleeve, hanging from a mini plastic hanger, as if returning from the dry cleaner's. The company loved how we turned the socks into "clothing." No one ever made a big deal of men's socks before—but as they say, if you have a need, fill it!

Antonovich

THESE PAGES
I created the visual identity for Antonovich, a well-known furrier who at the time was located in New York's Garment District. I made the name easier to read and pronounce—and more memorable—by breaking up the word phonetically and extending the line of the second "n" in "Anton." The font is exotic, foreign, and intimates luxury. It imparts a Russian flavor without faking the Cyrillic alphabet. The "Ah!" graphic was designed for a three-dimensional sign that was to appear in front of the company's retail shop on a highway in New Jersey.

THESE PAGES
An interesting project came to us from Reemtsma, the German tobacco giant, which included that the assignment was to name and design several ranges of cigarettes for the military. These smokes would be cheaper and sold only at NATO bases around the world. It was most important that the packaging not look like other cigarettes that could be purchased in the civilian world. I distinguished four different kinds of cigarettes, *left from top*, with oversized letters "M," "L," "R," and "L," standing for "menthol," "lights," "regular," and "king-size lights," so that one could easily find one's favorite cigarette type. Since people in the military are always traveling, I made Traveler Cigarettes, *below*, a brand they could relate to by designing the package to resemble a passport. As they say, if you're going to borrow—or is it steal?—take it from the best. I always loved the work of German poster artist Ludwig Hohlwein, and carried this image of his, *opposite*, around in my head for years. Sorry, Ludwig.

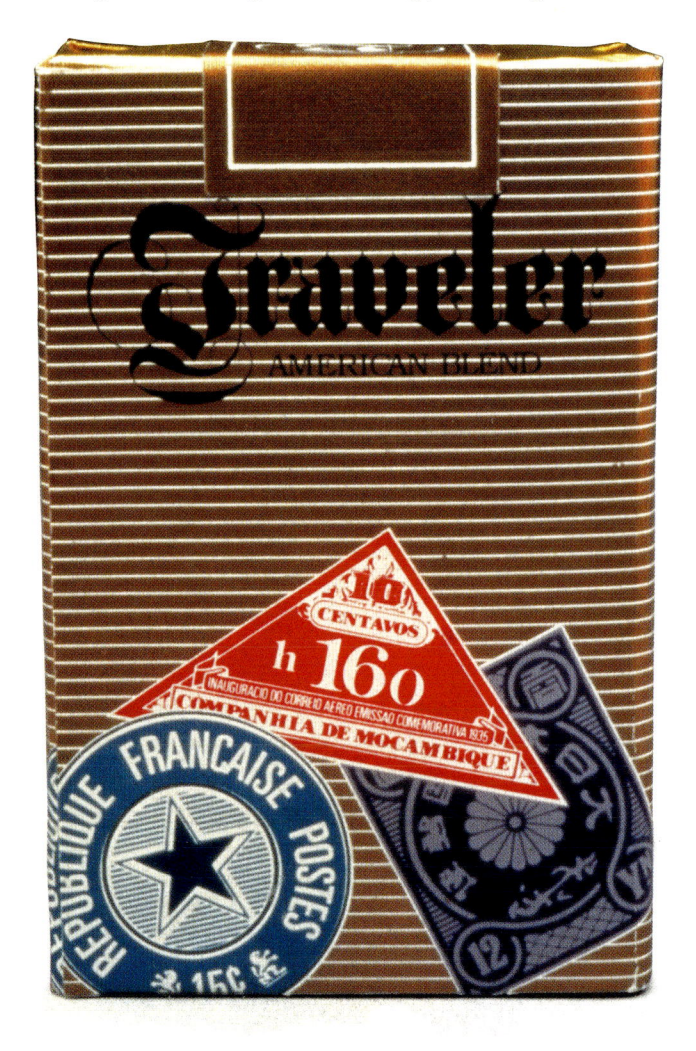

PARK
AVENUE

RIGHT
The elegant brand of a new candy product called Little Feasts was developed for Sarotti, a company that wanted to start a fancier line with higher price points. I did a lot of research on old Italian candy packaging from the early 1900s to create a brand-new old-fashioned–looking package.

BELOW
I designed the logos and packaging for Akzel Laboratories' line of pet deodorant products, including Kennel No.5, my favorite. The logos are all hand-lettered to incorporate animal tails.

Pretty

LITTLE FEASTS

LEFT
When Loft's, a low-end New York-based candy company, asked me to come up with a new logo, I suggested one with rounded and whimsical hand-lettering that conveyed fun and pleasure.

BELOW AND OPPOSITE
I designed the graphics and label for a line of clear soft-drinks branded American Pop, the five flavors distinguished only by the color of the round label on the bottle. When the soda got to the test market, it failed miserably. Everyone loved the packaging, which went on to win a couple of awards, but hated the taste of the drink. The aluminum foil label and neon letterforms are reminiscent of the California diner culture popular in the 1950s, as portrayed in the 1973 film *American Graffiti*.

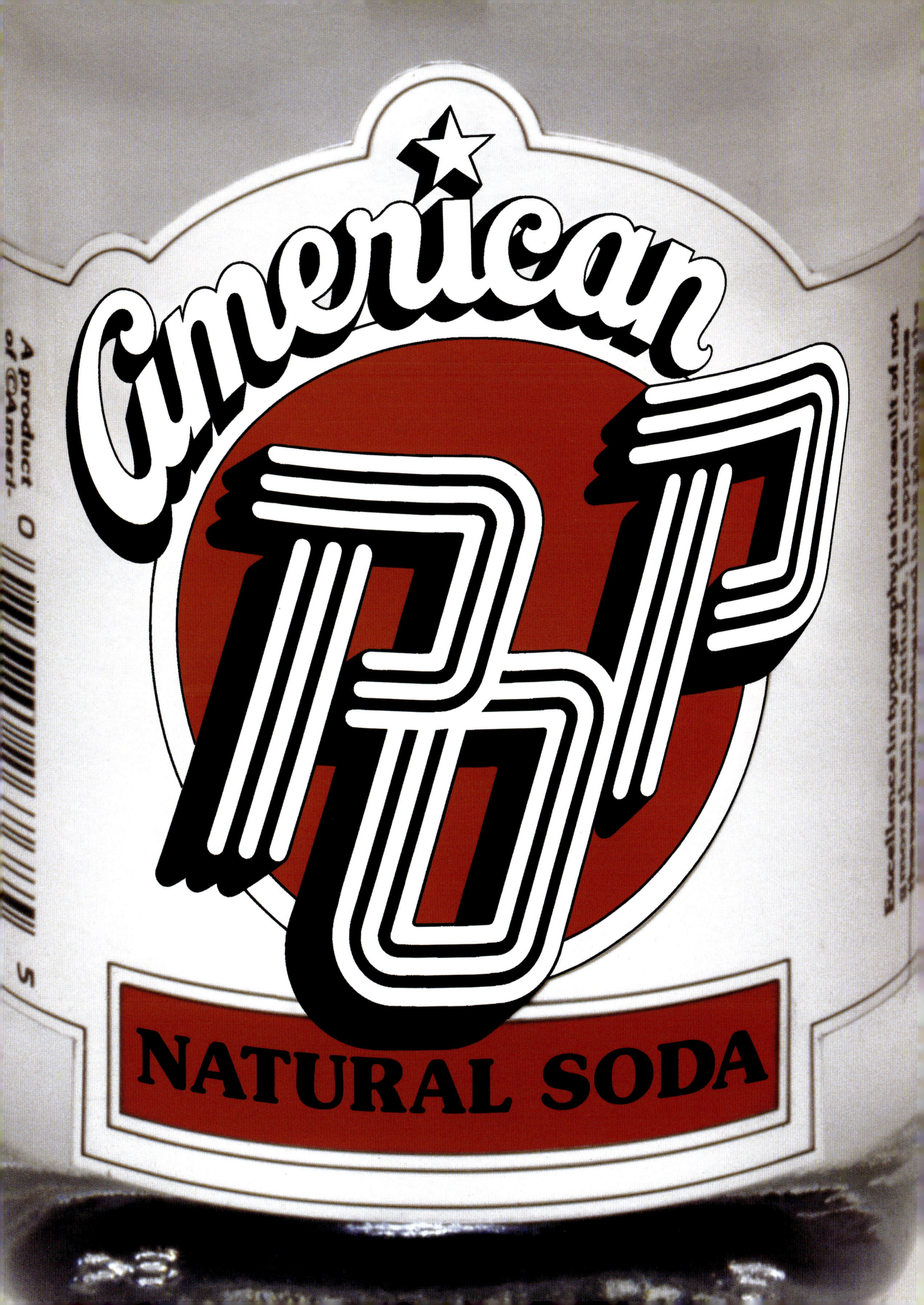
American
NATURAL SODA
A product

FOOD&WINE

D&W

ABOVE
In the late 1970s, a new food magazine arose to challenge *Gourmet,* the granddaddy of them all. *Food & Wine* was an upstart, a decidedly upscale and very sophisticated food magazine that eventually changed how food was presented and photographed. Jessica Weber, its first art director, asked me to create a sleek and sophisticated logo for the masthead. To make it modern, I decided to use an ampersand between the words. My first design, *above,* ran for four issues before the publisher asked for a slight revision, *top.* I had designed such a beautiful ampersand that it too closely resembled an "s," and people began referring to the magazine as *Food Swine.* Not a good thing.

OPPOSITE
My client wanted to upgrade the image of beer to a more classy beverage, suitable to be served at fancy dinner parties. I created a new bottle shape to closely resemble that of Champagne, and made the label black, which is usually extremely taboo for any food product. My client loved the design, and the beer was a hit.

Double Dark
Prior Beer
PRIOR BREWERY, PHILA., PA. & CLEVE., OH. CONTENTS 12

BELOW
One of the oldest women's magazines required a facelift. I did the covers, while Herb did the interiors. Because the magazine had a lot of type and photographs on its covers, I decided to keep the logo simple and clean using Futura, with a little nip and tuck.

Family Circle

OPPOSITE
I designed the packaging for the Kimberly-Clark Corporation's new line of extra-soft tissues. I saw a graphic opportunity in the spaces of the "O" and "Q," so I built the other letters around those by stacking and condensing them.

OVERLEAF
Rush, a New York-based contemporary dance troupe, asked me to create a new logo. I tried to capture the movement and grace of a dancer by rounding out the letters and angling them forward.

SOFTIQUE

RUSH
DANCE COMPANY

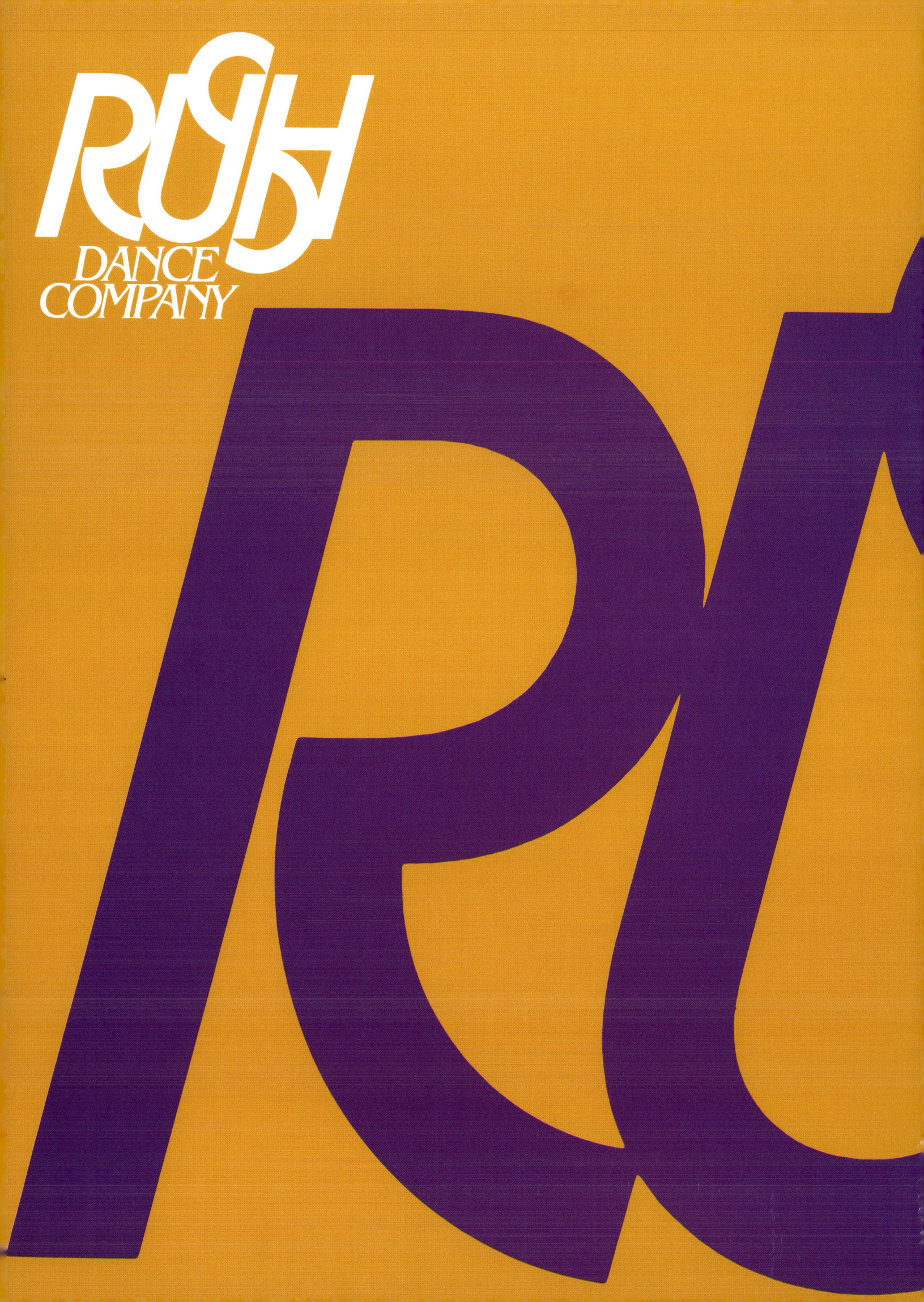

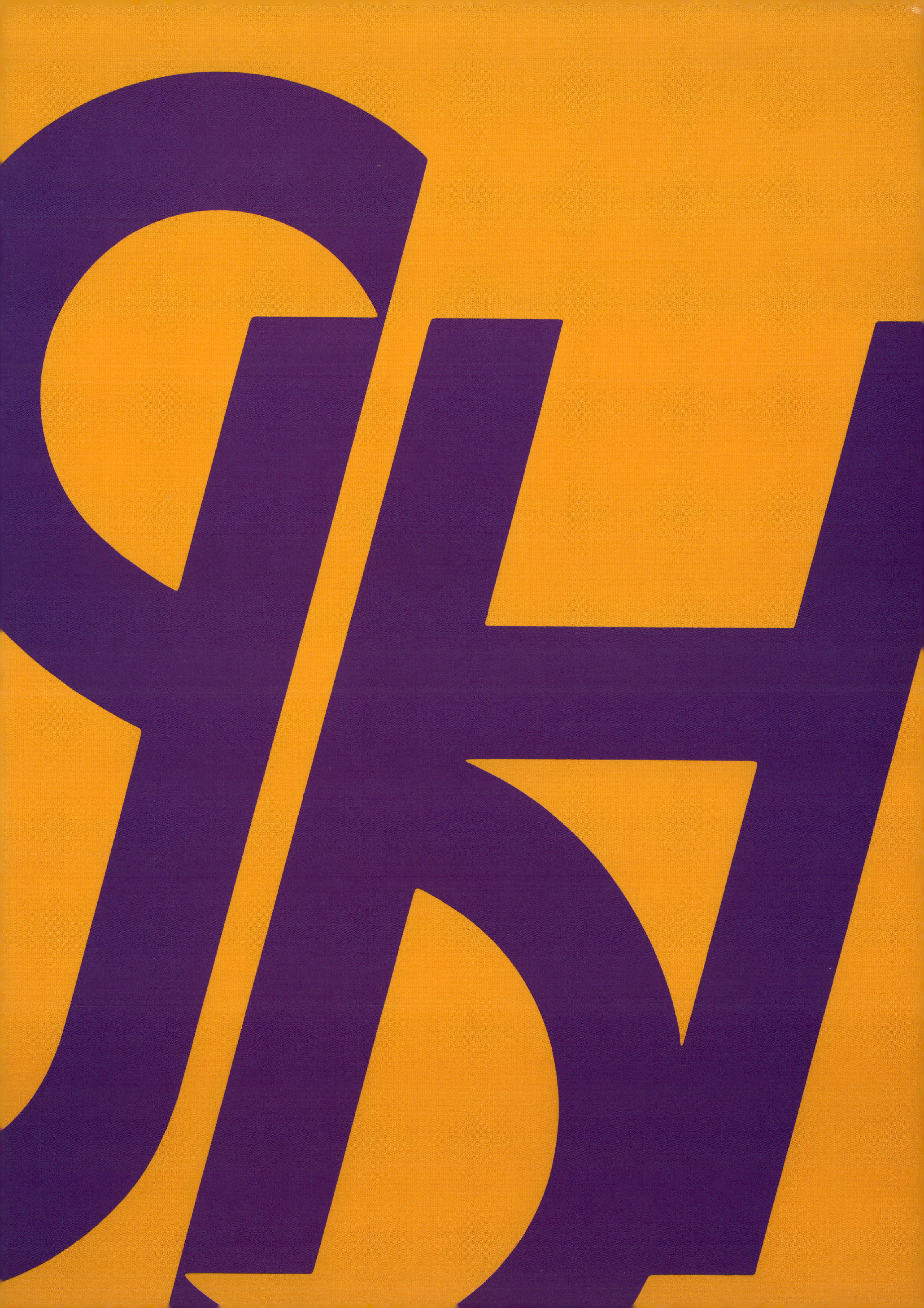

INDEX

Addison, 25
Adelphi University, 144
Akzel Laboratories, 156
Alan Peckolick Graphic Design, 22–23
American Pop, 48, 158
American Savings Bank, 133
annual reports: AT&T, 78, 79; Grupo Industrial Alfa, 66, 124; New York City Partnership & Chamber of Commerce, 77; Oppenheimer Capital, 121, 122
Antonovich, 153
ASICS, 150
AT&T, 78, 79
The Atlantic Gallery, 102

The Band, 95
Baruch College, 139, 143
Bass, Saul, 19–21, 93
Beaver, Allan, 145
book jacket design: *The American Political Dictionary*, 86; *Beards*, 35; *The Bedside Book of Bastards*, 35; *Culture Is Our Business*, 75; *The Generals*, 84; "*Get That Nigger Off the Field!*", 75; *Hess*, 71; *The Nothing Book*, 39; *The Progress of the Protestant*, 73; *The Shaping of the Arabs*, 73; *Stomping the Blues*, 109; *The World from My Window*, 86, 87
brochure and catalog design: Ebasco Services, 116; Kaufman Astoria Studios, 93; Neenah Paper Company, 40, 43; Polish short-film festival, 102; Type Directors Club annual, 63
building signage, 55, 57, 93, 139, 153

Carnese, Tom, 23, 97
Center for Jewish History, the 55
Chermayeff, Ivan, 6–8
Chwast, Seymour, 24
City College of New York, 143
Columbia House, 101
Container Corporation of America, 55
Corporate Annual Reports, 25
Craft, Kinuko Y., 60

DiSpigna, Tony, 37, 43, 65
Dorfsman, Lou, 8

Ebasco Services, 116
18 Bank, 135
expressive typography, 14–15, 33

Film League, 97
Fujita, S. Neil, 8

Geismar, Tom, 7
Genocide (film), 92
Ginzburg, Ralph, 80
Goin' South (film), 95
Goodman, Art, 20
graphic expressionism, 14
Great Ideas of Western Man, 55
greeting card design, 37
Grupo Industrial Alfa, 124
Guggenheim Museum, 104

Hathaway Shirt Man campaign, 75
Helena Rubenstein Company, 50–51
Heller, Steven, 15
Herb Lubalin, Inc., 65
Hiroshima Peace Memorial Museum, 84
Hohlwein, Ludwig, 154

International Typeface Corporation (ITC), 15

The Japan Society, 139
Jessica Weber Design, Inc., 25, 144
Juilliard School, 144, 145

Kator, Al, 18
Kaufman Astoria Studios, 93
Kimberly-Clark Corporation, 162

La Motta, Joseph M., 121
The Last Waltz (film), 95
Levine Huntley Schmidt & Beaver, 145
Little Feasts, 156
Loft's Candy, 158
logos, 46, 53, 59; Adelphi University, 144; Akzel Laboratories, 156; American Savings Bank, 133; *American Stage* magazine, 106; ASICS, 150; The Atlantic Gallery, 102; Baruch College, 139; Columbia House, 101; 18 Bank, 135; *Family Circle* magazine, 162; The Film Channel (Star Channel), 101; *Food & Wine* magazine, 160; *Genocide* (film), 92; Helena Rubenstein Company, 50–51; Juilliard School, 144, 145; *The Last Waltz* (film), 95; Loft's Candy, 158; Nassau Community College, 143; New York University (NYU), 145; *One-Trick Pony* (film and album), 97; Phoenix House, 53; Revlon Inc., 150; Rush dance company, 162; *Short Eyes* (film), 97; Time Equities, Inc., 133; Toes Clothes, 150; *Weekend at Dunkirk* (film), 97; *Zeitung*, 53
Lois, George, 9
Lubalin, Herb, 8, 9, 14–16, 21–24, 33, 80, 81, 84, 106, 150
Lubalin, Peckolick Associates, 9
Lubalin Smith Carnese, 23
Lubalin Smith Carnese & Peckolick (LSC&P), 23
Lustig, Alvin, 8

magazines: *American Stage*, 106; *Fact*, 80; *Family Circle*, 162; *Food & Wine*, 160; *Idea*, 65; *The New Leader*, 81
McCann Erickson, 20
McGraw-Hill, 102
McLuhan, Marshall, 75
Mobil Corporation, 104
Mucha, Alphonse, 51
Museum of American Folk Art, 104

Nassau Community College, 143
Neenah Paper Company, 40, 65

New York Art Directors Club, 60, 65
New York University (NYU), 145
Nichols, Mike, 106
Nicholson, Jack, 95
Nixon, Pat, 87
Nixon, Richard M., 87

Ogilvy & Mather, 75
One-Trick Pony (film and album), 97
Oppenheimer Capital, 121, 122
Os-Cal, 115

packaging design, 115, 154, 156, 158, 160, 162
Paper & Ink, 57
PBS, 104
Peckolick + Partners, 25
Peckolick, Alan: design philosophy, 29, 32–33; early life and education, 16–19; George Lois on, 9; Ina Saltz on, 14–29; Ivan Chermayeff on, 6–8; Jan V. White on, 10–13; painting career, 27–29
Peckolick Design Consultants, 25
Peckolick Papers, 60
Phoenix House, 53
political statements, 84, 87
poster design, 30, 55, 60, 65, 84, 95, 97, 104
Prior Beer, 160
proprietary typefaces, 143
Pushpin Lubalin Peckolick, 24

Reemtsma, 154
Revlon Inc., 150
Rush dance troupe, 162

Saltz, Ina, 14–29
Sarotti, 156
Schwartzman, Arnold, 92
Scorsese, Martin, 95
Short Eyes (film), 97
signage, 55, 57, 93, 139, 153
Simon, Paul, 97
Simon Wiesenthal Foundation, 92
Smith, Ernie, 23, 65
Sudler & Hennessey, 8, 21

Time Equities, Inc., 133
Time Warner, 101
Traveler cigarettes, 154
typeface design, 143

U&lc, 15

Weber, Jessica, 25, 160
Weekend at Dunkirk (film), 97
White, Jan V., 10–13
Whitney Museum of American Art, 104
Wiener Werkstätte design movement, 43
Wisconsin Dairy Council, 59
Woodpecker Products, 59

Zeitung, 53

BIOS

A founding principal of Chermayeff & Geismar & Haviv, **IVAN CHERMAYEFF** is a designer, painter, and illustrator whose work has been exhibited throughout the United States, Europe, and Asia. He is a Benjamin Franklin Fellow of the Royal Society of Arts, a member of the Alliance Graphique Internationale, a Hall of Fame honoree of the Art Directors Club, and a visiting Professor at the School of Visual Arts. He was a member of the Board of the Museum of Modern Art for 20 years and was a past president of the American Institute of Graphic Arts.

The legendary **GEORGE LOIS** is acknowledged as the most creative, prolific advertising communicator of our time. George Lois is the only person in the world inducted into The Art Directors Hall of Fame, and The One Club Creative Hall of Fame, with a Lifetime Achievement award from the American Institute of Graphic Arts, a Herb Lubalin Award (from the Society of Publication Designers), as well as serving as a subject of the Master Series at the School of Visual Arts.

JAN V. WHITE, architect by training, graphic design consultant by trade, sculptor by avocation. Born in Prague, educated in England. Cornell and Columbia (architecture). After 13 years' art-directing architectural magazines at Time Inc., he started his publication design studio in Westport, CT. He soon found out that *why* design works was far more interesting than *how*, and that he could explain the writers' problems with the designers, while justifying the designers' frustrations with the editors. So he gave up real work and turned to pontificating, which was more fun—he could travel the world (and did). Consulting is not solving specific design problems (which is usually what clients expect), but revealing what the real problems are and explaining to the editor/designer teams why and how their solution might work. His business card says "Design consultant," but more accurately, "itinerant guru." He wrote streams of articles and a dozen books on publishing including his classic *Editing by Design,* now in its 39th year and translated into languages that can't utilize our typography.

INA SALTZ is a professor of Art in Electronic Design and Multimedia at The City College of New York. For 25 years she was a Design Director for magazines including *Time's* International Edition, *Worth* and *Golf*. Saltz is currently principal of Saltz Design. She also writes and lectures frequently on topics relating to typography and editorial design for magazines such as *Graphis* and *STEP Inside Design*. Saltz is on the design faculty of The Stanford Professional Publishing Course.

CREDITS

Unless otherwise noted, all items in **Teaching Type to Talk** are from the collection of Alan Peckolick. Every effort has been made to locate the holders of copyrights. Any omissions will be corrected in future printings.

Page 29: Herb Fixler; Page 31: Photograph by Jessica Weber; Page 34: Houghton Mifflin Harcourt; Cover from *Beards* by Reginald Reynolds (Orlando: Harvest, 1976); Page 40: Courtesy McGraw-Hill; Pages 41-51: Special thanks to Neenah Paper Company; Page 53: Courtesy Phoenix House; Page 55: Special thanks to the Center for Jewish History; Page 60: Illustration by Chas. B. Slackman; Page 62: Special thanks to Art Directors Club; Illustration by Kinuko Y. Craft; Page 63: Special thanks to the Type Directors Club; Page 65: Special thanks to *Graphis*; Page 66: Photograph by Jay Maisel; Page 67: Illustration by Fred Otnes and Frank Moscati; Pages 70-71: Reprinted with permission of Scribner, a Division of Simon & Schuster, Inc.; Page 75: ©1972 by Ballantine Books, from *Culture Is Our Business* by Marshall McLuhan. Used by permission of Ballantine Books, an imprint of the Random House Publishing Group, a division of Random House, Inc.; Page 76: Special thanks to The Partnership for New York City, Inc.; Page 81: Special thanks to Myron Kolatch; Page 86: From Plano. The American Political Dictionary, 9th Edition ©1993 Wadsworth, a part of Cengage Learning, Inc. Reproduced by permission. www.cengage.com/permissions; Pages 90-91: Special thanks to the Simon Wiesenthal Center, Inc.; Pages 92-93: Special thanks to Kaufman Astoria Studios; Page 95: *Goin' South* ©1978 by Paramount Pictures Corporation. All Rights Reserved; Goin' South Courtesy of Paramount Pictures; Page 96: Photograph by Carl Fischer; Page 97: Licensed By: Warner Brothers, Entertainment Inc. All Rights Reserved.; Page 100: Used with permission of Showtime Networks, Inc.; Pages 104-105: Courtesy ExxonMobil; Pages 108-111: *Stomping the Blues* by Albert Murray. Copyright ©1976 by Albert Murray; Page 116: Special thanks to Adelphi University; Page 117: Special thanks to Allan Beaver & Robert Reitzfeld; Page 117: Courtesy the Juilliard School; Page 118: Special thanks to Nassau Community College; Page 119: Special thanks to The City College of New York.; Page 122: ©Baruch College/The City University of New York. Pages 124-125: Special thanks to Eighteenth Bank; Page 128: Special thanks to Time Equities, Inc.; Pages 134-137: Special thanks to Joseph M. La Motta; Pages 144-145: Photograph by Frank Moscati; Page 148: Courtesy Revlon; Page 150: Special thanks to ASICS Corporation; Pages 152-153: Courtesy Antonovich; Page 160: Logo courtesy of *Food & Wine*; Page 162: Special thanks to *Family Circle*; Page 163: Trademarks of Kimberly-Clark Worldwide, Inc. ©KCWW, used with permission; Pages 164-165: Special thanks to Rush Dance Company.

ACKNOWLEDGMENTS

Beginning this list must be Herb **Lubalin**, who was my mentor, collaborator, and finally my partner. Without Herb's influence in my life, I would not be the designer I am today.

I would like to thank Suzanne **Slesin,** the publisher, and everyone at Pointed Leaf Press for seeing the potential of this book, and for her steadfast encouragement during the production of this book.

To Ivan **Chermayeff**, George **Lois,** and Jan V. **White** for contributing to the Foreword, and Ina **Saltz** for her introduction.

To Dominick **Santise, Jr.,** who collaborated with me and did such a superb job designing page after page, while I made edits and continuous changes. A designer of such gracious patience and good humor is indeed a rarity, and Nick gets the gold medal.

To Susan **Marber**, permission sleuth par excellence, who began the paper trail.

To the team at Jessica Weber Design, Inc., for its generous help. First to Jessica **Alonzo**, my stalwart permissions research detective, who followed the trail begun by Susan **Marber**, who never gave up finding long-lost clients and made order out of editorial chaos. To Tyler **Bush** and Justine **Hirshfeld**, for putting up with my eccentricities with patience, diplomacy and, always, good cheer.

To my special friend Andree **Abecassis,** literary agent extraordinaire, for her most generous and gracious help throughout the production of this book.

To Lisa **Darms** and Marvin **Taylor** at the Fales Library at New York University.

Thanks also go to the gifted designers, photographers, illustrators, and clients with whom I was privileged to have worked during my career.

©2013 Alan Peckolick
All rights reserved under international copyright conventions. No part of this book may be reproduced, utilized, or transmitted in any form or by any means, electronic or mechanical, including photocopying, recording, or by any information storage and retrieval system, or otherwise, without permission in writing from the publisher.

Inquiries should be addressed to:

Pointed Leaf Press, LLC.
136 Baxter Street,
New York, NY 10013
www.pointedleafpress.com

Pointed Leaf Press is pleased to offer special discounts for our publications. We also create special editions and can provide signed copies upon request. Please contact info@pointedleafpress.com for details.

Printed and bound in China
First edition
10 9 8 7 6 5 4 3 2 1
Library of Congress
Control Number: 2012951385
ISBN: 978-1-938461-06-4

If you liked this, you'll love the good stuff…

Alan Peckolick
Alan Peckolick
Alan Peckolick
Typographica
Speaking
Alan Peckolick
pographica
Speaking
Alan Peckolick